Don't Misunde

A Comedy

Patrick Cargill

Samuel French – London
New York – Sydney – Toronto – Hollywood

DON'T MISUNDERSTAND ME

First presented on 1st May, 1984, at the Thorndike Theatre, Leatherhead, with the following cast:

Margery	Josephine Tewson
Charles	Patrick Cargill
Robert	Terence Longdon
Jaynie	Victoria Burgoyne
The Girl	Louisa Rix

The play directed by Roger Clissold
Designed by Tim Shortall

The action of the play takes place in Charles and Margery Fleminge's house near Richmond, Surrey

Time—the present

ACT I   A Friday evening in late June
ACT II   One hour later

ACT I*

The living-room of Margery and Charles Fleminge's house near Richmond, Surrey. It is a Friday evening in late June

The room was obviously once two rooms that have been knocked into one, as revealed by the projection of what remains of the dividing wall, and the RSJ in the ceiling

The right hand wall consists of two large windows which reach almost to the ground. The back wall has two sets of sliding doors, permanently open, which are separated by a wall containing the remains of the dividing wall mentioned above. The left hand wall contains french windows, downstage of centre, which lead into the garden. Above these is the door to the dining-room. Another small wall is below the french windows. There is a sofa, with an armchair either side. In front of one of the windows is a desk and chair. There is a sofa-table behind the sofa, and largish tables in front of the window and below the french windows. Occasional tables complement the furniture. There are wall lights in between the windows, and in the central back wall. Paintings on the walls, and ornaments on the larger tables, are in abundance. There is an air of comfort and moderate wealth in the whole room. There is a lamp on one of the tables. Through the two sets of open sliding doors can be seen the passage which runs along the back. Out of sight of the audience are the front door and the door to a cloakroom. The first few treads of a staircase can be seen. A hall rack and table might be visible between the staircase and the front door. There is a door to the kitchen, which, when open, reveals a kitchen dresser

Note: Only the right hand sliding door is practical

At the rise of the CURTAIN *the stage is empty*

Margery Fleminge an attractive woman in her middle forties who even contrives to look elegant in the apron she is wearing, enters from the kitchen. She carries a few pieces of cutlery

Margery (*calling*) Charles! (*She crosses to the stairs and calls upstairs*) Charles! Do you know what time it is? Charles!

Margery disappears along the passage, then reappears

Oh, where is the idiotic man!

Margery exits into the dining-room

Charles Fleminge appears through the french windows. He is a little older than his wife, but out of the same stable. He is carrying secateurs and a bunch of roses, around which is wrapped a T-shirt

---

*N.B. Paragraph 3 on page ii of this Acting Edition regarding photocopying and video-recording should be carefully read.

Charles That is the very last time I cut any blasted roses.

Margery enters from the dining-room

I'm lacerated from head to foot.

Margery I told you to wear the gardening gloves.

Charles I should have worn a suit of armour.

Margery (*indicating the sofa table*) Put them on the table.

Charles Lacerated!

Margery I think Aunt Mabel's vase would be rather nice.

Margery exits to the kitchen

Charles Wretched things! Just like women—look beautiful, smell divine, and bloody hard to handle!

Margery reappears with a vase and proceeds to arrange the roses carefully

Margery Do you know what time it is?

Charles About a quarter of an hour later than when you last asked me.

Margery It's five to seven.

Charles (*checking with the clock on the desk*) Exactly right.

Margery But they said they'd be here at seven, and you haven't even changed.

Charles (*sitting in an armchair*) You don't think I'm going to dress up for my own brother do you?

Margery You've cut some of these rather short.

Charles Even though he is bringing his new wife.

Margery And these secateurs live in the garden shed.

Charles They asked if they could see the inside of the house for a change.

Margery (*handing the secateurs to Charles*) Well, they've had their little treat. Now they can go back home.

Charles Anyway, knowing Robert, he'll be wearing what he considers is the "with-it gear" for the middle-aged man. Makes him look like mutton dressed as a lamb cutlet. (*He indicates his cardigan*) I shall simply take this off and put on my blazer.

Margery And wash your hands and brush your hair, I hope.

Charles Yes, matron. And I shall go to the lavatory.

Margery Do you suppose there's the remotest chance Robert's new wife will be an improvement on his last?

Charles Anything would be an improvement on his last. If Quasimodo's half-caste mother-in-law were to walk in, she'd be *Venus di Milo* compared to Abigail.

Margery Poor Abigail.

Charles Abigail! What a name, for a start.

Margery She was hardly responsible for that.

Charles How Robert put up with her for however many years it was, I shall never know. And look at the kids she presented him with! Two founder members of St Trinians, and a refugee from a remand home.

Margery Poor Abigail.

Charles Every time they call me "Uncle" in public I curse my parents for having given me a brother.

Margery Where are they now?
Charles With Abigail, terrorizing the citizens of Weston-super-Mare.
Margery Poor Abigail.
Charles And do stop saying "Poor Abigail".

Charles is about to go out of the french windows with the secateurs. Margery hands him the T-shirt

Margery You can take this back as well.
Charles Ah, yes. What was this perfectly good vest doing in the garden shed? It's eminently wearable.
Margery Well, if the caption fits, wear it. (*She turns it round and the caption reads, "Get with it, Daddy-O"*)
Charles Very funny! (*He snatches the T-shirt*)

Charles exits to the garden

Margery has completed the flower arrangement and now contemplates where to place the vase. She finally elects the sofa-table. She glances at her watch

Margery Oh, my God! It can't be! (*She looks at the clock on the desk, then runs to the french windows*) Charles! It's seven o'clock exactly. (*She starts to busy herself with a duster*)

Charles enters from the garden

Charles I wish the garden shed would shut exactly.
Margery And you should have come in the back way.
Charles I see no point in having doors to the garden if one's got to go in and out the back way.
Margery Dirt on the floor.

There is a pause while Charles surveys the roses

Charles Are you going to put those roses on the desk?
Margery No, I'm going to leave them there.
Charles They'd look much nicer on the desk.
Margery I don't agree.
Charles Much better background. And you can see them when you're sitting down. They'll look much nicer on the desk.
Margery They're staying there.
Charles Have it your own way.
Margery I will, dear.

Charles moves to the desk and takes a cigarette from the box

Do you know, I dusted all this furniture only this morning, and it's filthy again already.
Charles Pollution. It'll be the death of us all before long. (*He lights a cigarette*)
Margery (*at the sofa table*) Do you think she'll be forty and frumpish?
Charles Who?
Margery Jane.
Charles Jane who? (*He picks up a newspaper and sits at the desk*)

Margery Jane. Robert's new wife. Jane!

Charles Oh, Jane. No, my guess is she'll be twenty and dolly—to blot out the memory of Abigail.

Margery Poor ...

Charles NO!!! Besides, if she was forty and frumpish he would never have spent the money on a three-week honeymoon in Portofino.

Margery Where exactly is Portofino? (*She dusts the desk*)

Charles I've no idea, darling. But it's somewhere everybody thinks it's smart to go; which of course it isn't, because the people who made it smart can't afford to go there any more, and the hordes that used to go to Blackpool can.

Margery Oh, don't get on your social revolution kick again, for Heaven's sake.

Charles Nothing of the sort, I am blissfully looking forward to the day when Blackpool will be the "in" place for the chosen few. Much better beach.

Margery How do you know, if you've never been to Portofino?

Charles I've never been to Blackpool either.

Margery What a pity the children are in France. They'd have liked to have met Jane.

Charles I think it's a good thing they are in France. I've always said this exchange holiday plan for students was a good thing.

Margery No, you haven't. You said it was a rotten idea because we've got to have the French children here next year.

Charles We can always get out of that—chicken pox or something.

Margery No, we cannot! That would be disgusting.

Charles I like being disgusting sometimes.

Margery No comment. (*She finishes dusting*) Well, that's all I'm going to do in here. I hope everything's ready. Did you put the drinks out?

Charles Yes, dear.

Margery And the soda?

Charles Yes, dear.

Margery And the wine in the fridge?

Charles Yes, dear. (*He pauses*) What wine?

Margery (*stopping at the kitchen door*) What do you mean, what wine? The wine you bought on the way back from the office.

Charles I'm afraid you're going to believe this only too well, Margery, but I forgot to buy the wine.

Margery Oh, Charles! The only thing I asked you to do.

Charles I'll go right now.

Margery Everywhere's closed. Really, this is too bad of you.

Charles What about the Indian place?

Margery Indian place? It's wine we want, not chapattis.

Charles No, the Indian delicatessen. It's just by ...

Margery Oh, that. I never go there, they're too expensive. But you're right, they will be open.

Charles Of course they will; they never close. Give me some housekeeping.

Margery Don't bother, I'll do it. There are some things I need for a cake I'm making anyway. Thank Heaven for little Indians.

Charles Yes, we've got a lot to be grateful to Gandhi for.

Margery I'll wait until they've arrived and then pop out. It'll relieve me from watching you drool over Robrt's new wife. You'll have to do the potatoes, though, or we won't get dinner until midnight.

Charles I will do the potatoes—that I promise.

Margery exits into the kitchen, taking off her apron. She leaves the door open

Charles wanders about. The phone rings

Margery dashes back in, carrying a shopping bag

Margery I'll get it!

But Charles is nearer the phone and answers it. Margery freezes

Charles (*into the phone*) Hello. Who? ... What's that? ... Who's that speaking? ... I can't understand a word you're saying.

Margery (*apprehensively*) Who is it?

Charles Some ass talking gibberish.

Margery Let me. (*She takes the receiver*) Hello ... Oh, 'ello ... *Comment?* ... *Ah, mais oui ... absolument.* (*To Charles*) It's the children, ringing from France.

Charles (*pleased*) Oh!

Margery They've reversed the charges.

Charles (*not so pleased*) Oh.

Margery (*into the phone*) Hello? Louisa? ... Hello, darling, how are you both? ... We were talking about you at breakfast ... What? ... Is it? ... Yes, I'm sure it is ... It's quite good here, too. Lots of sunshine. (*To Charles*) The weather.

Charles Really?

Margery (*into the phone*) How are you both? ... Oh, I'm so glad, darling. We've got Uncle Robert and his new ... What? No, it hasn't rained for days.

Charles The weather again! (*He wanders away, muttering at the cost of the call*)

Margery How's the French coming along? ... I said, how's the French ... What? Oh, we're fine ... Yes, he's fine, too ...

Charles Let me.

Margery Here he is ... What? ... I said, here he is ...

Charles (*taking the phone*) Louisa?

Margery Terrible line.

Charles *Ah, ma cheri. Et comment allez-vous ce soir, hein?* ... *Quoi? Je dit, comment allez-vous* ... I am not speaking Italian!

Margery (*taking the phone again*) Louisa? It's Mummy again.

Charles (*marching away*) I was very good at French.

Margery Yes, of course he knows you were joking.

Charles One of my best subjects.

Margery No, I couldn't understand him, either.

Charles Don't be so ridiculous!

Margery And how are Monsieur and Madame Branchard? ... Good. And

the children? ... I'm so glad ... they've what? ... Who's gone away? ...
(*With an anxious look at Charles*) Monsieur and Madame Branchard have
gone away for the weekend? ... And you and the children are doing for
yourselves. Oh, how lovely for you, darling. And what are you all doing at
the moment? ... You and Philippe are cosying it up in the garden ... and
Mark has gone nude bathing with Marie. Oh, I see.

Charles is stunned

Well, I hope everything will be ... I mean, I hope everything is all right ...
Charles Let me speak!
Margery (*waving him aside*) Well, that's lovely darling. Have a nice cosy ...
I mean, have a nice time ... Yes, see you on the twelfth ... Yes, I will ...
Goodbye, darling. (*She rings off*)

There is a pause

They send their love.
Charles I'm surprised they've got any to spare! Cosying it up and nude
bathing! Can this be our children doing such things?
Margery Well, they're certainly *your* children, if that's what you mean.
Charles I always said this exchange holiday plan for students was a mad
idea. They exchange too many things. It was the same when Robert went
to Juan-les-Pins. Got caught up with the most extraordinary girl. Turned
out to be a boy in the end.
Margery Aren't you over-reacting a bit? I'm sure it's not as bad as it
sounds.
Charles Well, it doesn't sound too good, does it?
Margery They can take care of themselves. They're seventeen. And in this
day and age ...
Charles (*sitting on the sofa*) I suppose it might be understandable for Mark,
but Louisa ... well!
Margery Perhaps, since they're twins, the right hand likes to do what the
left hand is doing.
Charles That sounds vaguely filthy.
Margery (*sitting*) In any case, I'd much rather they were outspoken about
it. It means the dangers are considerably less.
Charles Maybe ... but, seventeen! Why, at seventeen, I ...
Margery At seventeen you'd already had two affairs that *I* know of. You
told me about them to try and prove your manliness.
Charles Is that why you agreed to let me ...?
Margery Never mind! But, if nothing else, it taught me that you'd had
experience.
Charles Mere peccadillos. (*He goes to the french windows lighting a cigarette
as he goes*)
Margery Besides, I had every intention of you marrying me, so ...
Charles Oh, it was like that, was it?
Margery Yes, it was like that. Even though I had had to wait ten years for
you to propose.
Charles You know perfectly well I have always disapproved of people
marrying too young. I was fully mature when we married, and by then ...

Margery You had sown all your wild oats and were bored to death of boiling your own eggs.

Charles Have I ever denied it? (*He flicks ash into an ashtray*)

Margery exits to the hall to collect her cardigan, then re-enters

Margery Not often, so go and put on your blazer, and think how lucky you are to be drifting through your declining years with such an understanding companion. And please stop using all the ashtrays—I want them clean when the others arrive.

Charles I'll stop breathing too, if you like.

Margery Don't be silly, Charles. (*She picks up the ashtray on an occasional table and empties other ashtrays into it*)

Charles (*sitting in an armchair*) And don't go on at me about my declining years! Why, in a couple of months' time you'll be declining towards . . .

Margery In six months, actually.

Charles What's a month here or there?

Margery At your age, a month here is all right. A month there might lead to anything. (*She empties the ashtray into the wastepaper basket below desk*)

Charles (*alert*) A month where?

Margery There . . . anywhere. (*As she replaces the ashtrays, she recites*)
"I will travel o'er the while,
To mystic bay and tropic isle.
To havens blue, to pastures green.
To lands where man has never been."

(*Rather pointedly*) Or, of course, to New York.

Charles Oh, my God! You're not still going on about New York?

Margery Not really. You've got over whatever it was that happened there, but it does prove my point.

Charles How many hundreds of times must I tell you, nothing happened there. My fortnight in New York was extended by two weeks because of business.

Margery That really is rather old-fashioned, Charles.

Charles I don't care if it's antediluvian! Besides, you know perfectly well I normally go to New York at this time of year.

Margery Exactly. Then why did you go earlier this year?

Charles What do you mean?

Margery Normally, you go about this time—the end of June, the beginning of July. Why, this year, did you go in mid-April?

Charles Because it was more convenient.

Margery Exactly!

Charles For the company!

Margery Well, it certainly wasn't more convenient for me. In fact, it was very inconvenient.

Charles What?

Margery However, I suppose, in a way, I should be happy for you.

Charles Happy for me? Why?

Margery Well, it gave you the opportunity to indulge in a little spring fever. And, let's face it, you don't have all that number of springs left in which to indulge, do you?

Charles (*rising*) I know it is a biological fact that the husband, more often than not, succumbs before the wife. But in your case, I think your sharp tongue will have slit your throat before I am ready to go. (*He walks away*)

Margery Then you must take care you don't give it cause to, mustn't you? Or you'll be back to boiling your own eggs again.

Charles (*to her again*) I have said it before, and I will now say it again—and for the last time—nothing happened in New York.

Margery Then how do you account for the starry eyes and the cat-with-the-top-of-the-milk look on your return?

Charles It's a very bracing place.

Margery Oh, come now, Charles! New York may be called many things, but never bracing.

Charles Well, I found it so. And before you start condemning the place too much, who was it got all starry-eyed over a certain New York tennis star?

Margery I don't know what you're talking about.

Charles Brad ... something or other. Brad ... Brad ...

Margery Oh, him. I met him twice—very briefly.

Charles And you've been going to Wimbledon every year since.

Margery I'm very fond of tennis.

Charles Oh, jolly hockey sticks! Anyone for tennis!

Margery Don't be imbecilic.

Charles Well, you'd better go to the outside courts this year—he must be in the over forty group now.

Margery I wouldn't have the faintest idea. Oh, my God! Look at the time! I'll have to go to the shops before they arrive. Is Robert always late?

Charles Always. He was a ten-month baby.

Margery dashes into the hall

The door slams

Bloody New York! Bloody Brad! Bloody hell! (*He deliberately, and very quickly, flicks from his cigarette into two ashtrays and stubs it out in a third. He then decides to move the roses to the desk, but, as he is crossing, they pop out of the vase and cascade on to the floor. He picks them up and shoves them untidily into the vase*

The doorbell rings. Charles puts the vase back on the sofa-table

Charles exits to the hall

Charles (*off*) Robert! At last!
Robert (*off*) Hello old boy.

Robert Fleminge enters carrying a handgrip and sets of golf clubs. He is younger than Charles, and more dashing. He is dressed as Charles described and is as flamboyant in manner. Charles enters behind him.

God, I have had the most bloody awful journey! How long does the rush-hour in London last, for heaven's sake?

Charles takes Robert's handgrip and puts it by the foot of the stairs

Charles It's always worse on Fridays—people getting away for the week-end.

Robert You mean they actually get a week-end—or do they just spend it driving?

Charles takes Robert's golf-clubs and puts them by his case at the foot of the stairs. He looks around for someone else

Charles Well, where is she?

Robert Who?

Charles The new wife—Jane.

Robert Jane. Oh, terribly sorry, old boy. Last minute, couldn't make it. Her mother fell over in the kitchen yesterday. Pissed, I shouldn't wonder. Nothing broken, but the old girl loves being ill, so Jane has gone up to look after them for a couple of days. All the way to Cambridge. She sends her "sorries".

Charles Oh, Margery will be disappointed. She was looking forward to me drooling all over her—Jane, I mean.

Robert And you would, old boy—absolute smasher! I can't tell you what it's like after Abigail.

Charles I don't think you have to.

Robert Yes, but apart from having someone who talks to you without snapping your head off, and is witty and amusing, and doesn't go around looking like the arse-end of a giraffe all the time, there's well, there's the other bit.

Charles What other bit?

Robert Oh, for God's sake, you know! It! That honeymoon, I can't tell you, old boy!

Charles Nice place, was it?

Robert I wouldn't know.

Charles Oh, I see.

Robert But really, old boy, I mean it—unbelievable! I didn't know I had it in me—or I'd forgotten what it was all about.

Charles Really. Drink?

Robert Scotch and water, thanks.

Charles exits to the dining-room

Robert wanders in the same direction

You know, I think every man should get married again after forty-five. It really does something for you. The whole thing is, men always remain virile, don't they? It's there, all the time, just waiting to be . . . satiated!

Charles enters, carrying two drinks

Charles I know what you mean. (*He shuts the dining-room door*)

Robert Well, of course you do. But believe me, Charles, when you're free to—what's the expression they use?—let it all hang out. I can't tell you, old boy!

Charles Please don't. Something very peculiar is happening to my adrenalin.

Robert Sorry about that. Cheers. (*He sits*)

Charles So I take it that Jane didn't turn out to be a boy in the end.

Robert What? A boy? Oh, that time in Juan-les-thing! Wasn't that chaotic! And do you know, the extraordinary thing was, old boy, I didn't suspect a thing until I was actually ...

Charles Yes, yes, you told me.

Robert Sorry. Adrenalin still bad?

Charles No, you've cured it. And don't use the ashtrays, Margery wants them clean when you arrive.

Robert (*puzzled*) And where is the old Marge? Upstairs or something?

Charles (*sitting*) No, she had to pop out. Forgot to buy the wine when she was out shopping.

Robert Of course, everything I've been saying doesn't apply to you and Marge. I mean, she's still absolutely smashing.

Charles (*musing*) Yes, yes she is. (*More firmly*) Yes, of course she is. Absolutely smashing. All the same, I have to admit to you that temptation is a hard thing to resist.

Robert Of course it is, old boy. You wouldn't be human if it wasn't.

Charles I know but ... well, you see I think you did the right thing. You were tempted, and when you realized the temptation had to be fulfilled — that it wasn't just a ... just a ...

Robert A flash in the pan? A pee in the sink?

Charles Something like that. When you realized that, you got divorced and went ahead.

Robert Not easy, but I did it. Mind you, you're right — I knew I had to.

Charles Yes, but you rather had things on your side, you know.

Robert How do you mean?

Charles Well, you had a bloody awful wife; your children took after her; and your home was like a pigsty.

Robert Oh, I wouldn't put it like that, old boy — it was much worse.

Charles (*rising*) Exactly. But, you see, in my case it was different.

Robert Your case? You mean you've *had* a case?

Charles Your use of the word "had" is unfortunate. You see, it was like this ... but don't breathe a word to Margery, will you? She doesn't know a thing about it, and if she did, she'd break her heart — and very possibly my neck! And, in any case, absolutely nothing happened — well, practically absolutely nothing happened.

Robert You've got my adrenalin going now. Can't you be more specific?

Charles At the very worst, it was just a mild flirtation.

Robert And at the very best?

Charles If you're going to be flippant ...

Robert Sorry. Go on.

Charles This is not easy, you know.

Robert It never is, old boy.

Charles As you know, I have to go to New York every year for the company.

Robert Yes, it must be ghastly for you.

Charles It usually is.

Robert I never know which street I'm in in New York — they all look the same.

Charles Do you want to hear my story or not?
Robert Sorry.
Charles This year I had to go a couple of months earlier—not that that has any bearing on the matter in the least.
Robert Then don't let's bother with it.
Charles Very well, Well, I'd done my fortnight's stint, and on the night before I was due to come home there was this sort of dinner party ...
Robert And at this sort of dinner party ...
Charles Exactly, there as this sort of ... creature.
Robert Four legs, or two?
Charles Two—very beautiful legs.

Both men fantasize for a moment

Robert Could I have another drink?
Charles I'll get the bottle.

Charles exits to the dining-room

Robert I suppose I know the rest of the story, but you may as well tell me. I presume it still has to be got off the old chest.

Charles comes back with a whisky bottle and a jug of water

Charles I suppose so, yes. Mind you, it's all over—completely finished. But I did do a rather rotten thing.
Robert You mustn't think of it as rotten, old boy—it's nature.
Charles No, not that! What I did was, I sent a cable to Margery saying I was kept in New York on business.
Robert That's a bit old-fashioned.
Charles That's what Margery said.
Robert I'm surprised she believed you.
Charles I sometimes wonder if she did. But the whole point is—absolutely shattered though I was by this delectable creature—any idea of giving up Margery and the kids was quite unthinkable. So, I did another rather rotten thing.
Robert Am I right this time?
Charles I told this ... this ...
Robert Delectable creature. Get on with it!
Charles I told her I was leaving on the Friday.
Robert What's rotten about that?
Charles (*sitting*) I actually left on the Thursday.
Robert What a rotten thing to do!
Charles I agree, I absolutely agree. But you see, in a way, I was doing it for Margery. Now, if I'd been married to Abigail ...
Robert (*rising*) Don't let's talk about Abigail, old boy. Life's hard enough as it is.
Charles No, but you know what I mean. I wasn't married to her, I was married to Margery. And there she was, that lovely Margery, and those two adorable kids ... (*Another thought suddenly strikes him*) Those kids. Are sexual habits hereditary?
Robert I haven't the faintest idea. Why?

Charles I dread to think what Louisa and Mark are getting up to in France, and it's just occurred to me that it might be all my fault.

Robert (*sitting*) Ye ... es. From all accounts, Father was a bit of a randy old sod.

Charles Yes ... which would account for you.

Robert And *you*.

Charles My God, yes. And me!

Robert Mind you, it doesn't follow that it's *all* your fault. I mean, if sexual habits are hereditary, then presumably the mother is responsible, too.

Charles Are you suggesting that our Mother was a randy old ...?

Robert Of course not! But you can't discount the fact that a certain measure of the responsibility must rest on Margery.

Charles Oh no, not Margery. No, it's impossible. On the other hand, she did let me ... before we were ... Oh no, she couldn't.

Robert I'm slightly confused.

Charles No, the only thing to do is not to give it another thought. I can be quite wrong about the kids. And as for myself ... I've had my fling, and it's all over and finished with. An unfortunate campaign that I deeply regret. I made my attack, carried out my skirmish, retreated in good order, and covered my tracks. I shall now dismiss the whole thing from my mind, and soldier on.

Robert That's the first time I've heard a mild flirtation described as a military assault. However, one point did interest me. You say you covered up your tracks.

Charles Completely. No telephone number, no forwarding address, nothing. She hasn't the faintest idea how to get in touch with me.

The front door bell rings

That'll be Margery back with the wine. (*He picks up the whisky bottle*) Better put this away.

Charles exits to the dining-room

(*Off*) Let her in, there's a good fellow.

Robert Don't you use front door keys in your house?

Charles enters

Charles Yes, but she likes me to open the door for her. Gives her a sense of authority. (*He starts emptying all the ashtrays*)

Robert And why are you emptying the ashtrays?

Charles I told you, she wanted them clean for when you arrived.

Robert But I have arrived.

Charles So you have.

The front doorbell rings again

For God's sake open the door! The potatoes!

Charles exits to the kitchen

Robert exits to the hall

Robert returns hurriedly a moment later, shutting the sliding door behind him

Charles enters from the kitchen at the same moment

Hello darling! The potatoes are doing fine. (*He realizes that Margery has not returned*) Oh.

Robert Charles, I hate to have to tell you this.

Charles She's forgotten the wine.

Robert Worse than that.

Charles She's dropped it.

Robert It isn't even she.

Charles What isn't even she?

Robert Well, it's she, but not that she. I think it's the other she.

Charles What the hell are you talking about?

Robert I think you underestimated the enemy's intelligence corps. (*He pulls open the sliding door*)

Jaynie is revealed behind the door. She is a vivacious American girl, barely in her twenties. She is as desirable in her clothes as she most certainly would be out of them. Her very noticeable week-end case is at her feet

Charles is stunned into a state of shock

Charles My God!! (*He prevents himself from collapsing by clinging on to Robert's arm*)

Jaynie Charlie! Surprise, surprise!

Robert (*to Charles*) Shock, shock.

Charles Jaynie! Is it you?

Jaynie Sure is, lover boy.

Charles Good gracious me. Good gracious me. Good gracious me.

Robert That's his version of three Hail Marys.

Charles Are you here? In England? In London?

Jaynie Well, if I'm not, that airline pilot sure needs a sharp talking to.

Charles hugs Robert even closer

Robert (*referring to the embrace*) Before you might jump to any unfortunate conclusion, I'm Charles's brother, Robert.

Jaynie Hi, Robert. I'm Jaynie.

Robert Yes, that's what I thought he called you. And since you've confirmed it, I think that answers all your questions, Charles. It is her; she is here; she is in England; and she is in London. All we need to establish now is whether she's here in the flesh. (*He disentangles himself from Charles and goes to Jaynie. He shakes her hand at the same time stroking her arm*) Yes, yes. Established. Flesh.

Charles Good gracious . . .

Robert You've done that. Why don't we all sit down.

Jaynie Great. (*She sits on the sofa*)

Robert sits besides Jaynie. Charles stands

You'll just never believe my luck, Charlie.

Robert Oh, I think he will. But I doubt if he'll believe his.

Jaynie About ten days ago, my father ... I told you about my father?

Charles I think you did mention him—some time—some place.

Jaynie (*to Robert*) He and Mamma—that's my mother—they don't get on too well, so they don't live together. They're ... well, they're ...

Robert Separated?

Jaynie Oh no, nothing like that. They're divorced.

Robert Oh, much more civilized.

Jaynie They were divorced when I was very young, and I hardly ever see him these days. But last April Mamma and I were in New York—we don't live there, you know, we live in California. Do you know Carmel?

Robert Carmel who?

Jaynie No, it's a place.

Robert Oh. I'm afraid I don't know it.

Jaynie Well, that's where we live—Mamma and me. My father lives in New York, which is why we were there, because Mamma wanted to see him—something to do with alimony or something. You know what I mean.

Robert I certainly do.

Jaynie And of course it was there that I met you, Charlie, wasn't it? At the *Blue Nightingale*. My, but you were having such a dull party, weren't you?

Charles Company get-togethers are rather staid.

Jaynie I was with an old school friend. You remember her, Charlie?

Charles Er ...?

Jaynie Hornrimmed glasses ... pigtails ... and a rather crooked face.

Robert I don't think he'd remember her.

Jaynie Any place, Charlie was so sweet. Do you know, he insisted on driving her all the way home.

Robert No!

Jaynie Yeah. Almost to New Jersey.

Robert Charles, you're a saint.

Jaynie And after that, we went on to ... where did we go on to after that, Charlie?

Charles The *Pink Partridge*, I think it was.

Jaynie That's right, the *Pink Partridge*.

Robert By Jove, you really were doing the birds that night, weren't you, Charles? And after that?

Jaynie After what?

Robert After the *Blue Nightingale* and the *Pink Partridge*?

Jaynie (*demurely*) Well, after that ...

Charles (*quickly*) But what brings you to England, Jaynie, and (*rather too pointedly*) for how long?

Jaynie But I never told you, did I?

Robert I think you started to, but somehow got sidetracked by our feathered friends.

Jaynie Well, about ten days ago, Daddy ... (*to Robert*) that's my father—I call him Daddy.

Robert Very appropriate.

Jaynie Ten days ago he phoned us in California and told us he was coming over to England—he comes over most years. When I was a little girl, Mamma used to say, "Well, your father's off on his little European jaunt again". For some reason she never seemed too pleased about it. In fact, I think it had a lot to do with their divorce, you know.

Robert Could be. Trips abroad can lead to all sorts of problems, can't they Charles?

Charles Please try not to interrupt, Robert.

Robert Sorry.

Jaynie Any place, it seems that when he saw me in New York he suddenly realized I wasn't a little girl any more.

Robert Very perceptive of him.

Jaynie Well, let's face it, I'm not, am I, Charlie?

Charles Well ... er ... well ... er ...

Robert Answer the lady, Charles.

Charles No ... no, you're not ... you're definitely not. I know that only too ... only too ... I mean ...

Jaynie Surely. And he was so pleased at the way I'd ...

Robert Shaped up?

Jaynie (*demurely*) You could put it that way.

Robert I certainly could!

Charles Robert, please.

Jaynie Any place, he felt he hadn't been all that good a father in the past, so he said he wanted to give me a treat and bring me with him. Well, you can imagine! I could have died—I could have just died.

Charles (*wishing she had*) Yes, I suppose you could.

Robert (*taunting again*) But she didn't.

Jaynie I can't stay as long as Daddy, but, at any rate, I'm here.

Robert Oh yes, that has been firmly established. You're here.

Charles (*dragging him towards the dining-room*) Robert, why don't you fetch some drinks? You'll find everything in there. Whisky, gin, vodka— vitriol.

Robert exits to the dining-room

Jaynie rushes to Charles and embraces him violently

Jaynie Oh, Charlie! It's been so long. I can't tell you!

Charles (*trying to disentangle himself*) Jaynie! Please!

Jaynie But Charlie ...

Robert enters from the dining-room

Robert Oops! Sorry!

Charles throws Jaynie from him

I just wondered if you wanted some ice—but I see that you do.

Robert exits to the kitchen

Charles (*sitting*) Ice. Yes, that would be nice, ice.

Jaynie But, Charlie, what happened? I called your hotel on the Friday and they said ...

Charles I'm terribly sorry, darling, I had to leave suddenly on the Thursday. But Jaynie, how the devil did you find out where I lived? Not that I'm not delighted to see you, because I'm not ... I am.

Jaynie Well, Daddy said he had to meet some people at the airport, and that he'd see me later at the Savoy Hotel. So, whilst I was waiting for a cab, there was this phone booth, and there was this directory, and ...
Charles There was my name and address.
Jaynie Right on! The only Fleminge with an E. Wasn't that just too lucky?
Charles Yes. My father added the E to distinguish us. I often questioned the wisdom of it.
Jaynie (*sitting on the arm of his armchair*) So I got the cabby to drop me off here. Aren't you pleased?
Charles Why, yes I ... I ...
Jaynie I only came to London to see you, Charlie. (*She embraces him again*)

Robert enters from the kitchen carrying an ice bucket

Robert Hang on! Won't be a minute!

Robert exits to the dining-room

Charles Jaynie, I think I ought to explain. You see, I've got my brother and his wife—that's my brother, getting the drinks ...
Jaynie Yeah, we met.
Charles Well, they're here, you see, staying here, and his wife ...

Robert enters with a tray of drinks. He puts it on the sofa table

Robert's wife ...
Jaynie She's here?
Robert My wife? No, she isn't. She ...
Charles She isn't—at the moment. But she will be ... very soon. (*For Robert's benefit*) She's gone to do some shopping—to get some wine. Hasn't she, Robert?
Robert (*puzzled*) Has she?
Charles Of course she has, Robert. You know she has.
Robert (*co-operating*) Oh yes, that's right, she has.
Charles (*crossing to Jaynie*) So you see ... and I'm *sure* Robert will agree with me, won't you Robert?
Robert Will I?
Charles Yes, of course you will.
Robert Yes, I expect so, yes.
Charles Well, there you are, you see.
Jaynie Where am I?

Charles looks to Robert for help

Robert (*to the rescue*) You're here.
Charles Yes, that's it—you're here. That's the whole point. You're here, and Robert's wife isn't. But she will be, and when she is, well ... well ... well ... (*He dries up*)
Robert I think what Charles is trying to say is, that when ... the wife ... returns, it's just possible that she might find it ... well ... strange.
Charles That's right, strange.
Robert Even ... odd.
Charles Yes, odd.

Robert Not quite . . .

Charles No, not at all "quite". (*He rushes to the window*) And she has a habit of returning very quickly, hasn't she, Robert?

Robert Yes, she has.

Charles In fact, she's quite the quickest returner I've ever known, so . . .

Jaynie Now listen. You don't have to explain. (*To Robert*) When Charlie was in New York he told me all about his divorce, and how you and your wife were the only ones who understood, and what great, great friends you were to him, and how, without you, he just wouldn't know what to do.

Robert (*to Charles*) Oh, you told her about *your* divorce?

Jaynie Yeah.

Charles Yeah . . . yes.

Robert And what great, great friends we were?

Jaynie That's right.

Charles Yes, that's right. And how (*pointing each word*) without you, I wouldn't know what to do!

Jaynie (*turning her back*) Absolutely.

Robert (*sotto voce*) And in what other ways did you impersonate me? (*He crosses to the desk*)

Charles (*desperate*) Robert! I . . .

Jaynie (*to Robert*) So it stands to reason that your wife isn't going to object to Charlie finding himself someone else who . . . well also . . . understands.

Robert I understand.

Charles Oh yes, he understands. He understands that it might be necessary to ease her into the situation. Say, tomorrow, or Sunday, or . . . some time next week, perhaps.

Jaynie I'm only here till Tuesday.

Charles Oh, good! . . . I mean, that will give us plenty of time to arrange something quite lovely, some other day. Won't it, Robert?

Robert Yes. Yes.

Charles Oceans of time. (*He has a sudden idea, and crosses to Robert*) And I've just remembered! You wanted to collect those tickets from the Savoy Theatre for tomorrow night, didn't you?

Robert Did I?

Charles Yes. We're going to see . . . what is it we're going to see, Robert?

Robert (*glancing at a nearby newspaper*) Er . . . the play.

Charles That's it! The play. We're going to see the play.

Robert (*seeing the title*) *The Day Before Yesterday*.

Charles No, no. Tomorrow night.

Robert That's the name of the play.

Charles *Tomorrow Night* is the name of the play?

Robert No, *The Day Before Yesterday* is the name of the play we're going to see tomorrow night.

Charles That's right, I knew it was something like that. And the Savoy Theatre is practically *in* the Savoy Hotel—that's where Jaynie is staying. So, you could drop her off there, couldn't you?

Robert Yes, that would be a great help, wouldn't it?

Charles Of course it would. (*He clasps Robert round the shoulders. To*

Jaynie) I told you I wouldn't know what to do without him. (*To Robert*)
Now, where's your car?

Robert Way the other side of the square.

Charles Fine—couldn't be nearer. (*To Jaynie*) Now, off you go, and I'll
phone you first thing in the morning when we've . . . when we've . . .

Robert Eased the wife into the situation.

Charles That's right.

Jaynie (*reluctant*) Well, I suppose it might be wiser.

Robert Much wiser.

Charles Oh, much, much wiser, I assure you.

Jaynie Before I go, do you think I could just . . . freshen up?

Charles Freshen up?

Robert You know. (*He bends his knees*)

Charles Oh! Yes, of course I do. There's a downstairs one next to the front
door. Meanwhile, I'll just wash up these glasses.

Jaynie But we haven't used them.

Charles I know, but they're filthy, anyway. (*Rounding on Robert*) Really,
Robert! How could you have brought out such filthy glasses!

Robert Silly of me.

Jaynie exits to the hall

I should have ground them up and put them in your dinner!

Charles What are you . . .? Dinner! Oh my God, the potatoes!

Charles moves to kitchen, but Robert stops him

Robert You've dropped me in it, haven't you?

Charles What do you mean?

Robert You've dropped me right in it! Not only am I now married to your
wife, but I've got to drive your concubine all the way to the Savoy under
the pretext of collecting some tickets for a show we're not even going to!

Charles I'll take you to it some time, I promise.

Robert Thank you very much!

Charles Look, there's no time to be lost. Go and fetch the car and get her
out of here as quickly as you can. Whatever happens, don't let Margery
see her. If necessary, fling a coat over her head.

Robert We don't have to kidnap the girl, surely.

Charles (*fiercely*) I'd like to . . . I'd like to . . .!

Robert I think you've done that already.

Charles Done what?

Robert Mild flirtation! You had it off with her, didn't you?

Charles Don't be crude.

Robert You—the pure one of the family! A zonking great affair—that's
what you had in little old New York.

Charles You know nothing about it.

Robert That's where you're wrong, dear brother, I think I know everything
about it. You innocent-looking ones are always the randiest.

Charles I beg your pardon!

Robert A zonking great, romping great, rollicking great AFFAIR!

Robert exits to the hall. Charles, slightly shattered, exits to the kitchen

Jaynie enters

Jaynie I say, Charlie ... (*seeing no one*) Oh, I say ...!

Margery enters suddenly, carrying a shopping bag and two bottles of wine. She calls as she enters

Margery Who left the front door wide open?

Both women are now in the living-room and confront each other

Oh. I beg your pardon.

Jaynie That's quite all right. You must be Mrs Fleminge.

Margery Margery, that's right. And you, of course, must be Jane.

Jaynie Jayne? Oh, it's funny me being called that again. Everyone knows me as Jaynie.

Margery (*putting down her basket and wine*) Do they? Then Jaynie it shall be. How do you do, Jaynie?

Jaynie Hi.

They shake hands

Margery (*as she takes her cardigan off*) It's awful the way people bastardize names, isn't it? I went through torture at school. I was known as Marge; Margie; Margarine. One particularly loathesome brat used to go the whole hog and call me Cooking Fat. Since her name was Primrose, I used to retaliate by calling her Dandelion.

Jaynie I quite like Jaynie.

Margery Come to think of it, so do I. Now, come and sit down Jaynie. I've heard so much about you.

Jaynie Is that so? I didn't think ...

Margery Oh, yes. Charles and I ... By the way, where are they both?

Jaynie Well, Robert has gone to get the car. It seems it's way the other side of the square.

Margery Parking round here can be appalling, but I think he'll find a space all right now. It must have been him who left the front door open.

Jaynie Oh gee, so it must.

Margery Not to worry—there's nothing worth stealing here anyway. Now, how about a drink?

Jaynie Well, as a matter of fact ...

Margery I hope the glasses are clean. (*She examines one*) Ah, yes, perfect. Now, what will it be?

Jaynie Well, you see, Charles was going to ...

Margery My dear, if we wait for him we'll die of dehydration. Oh, I see he's been at the roses again. (*She starts to re-arrange them*) He really is quite extraordinary. He can't bear picking them, and yet once they're in the vase he won't leave them alone. Look at them! Now, there's whisky, gin ...

Jaynie Look, I don't wish to be a nuisance, but I asked to freshen up and Charles showed me the powder room downstairs and, well, there's no towel.

Margery Oh, good Lord! Didn't I put one there? How maddening of me.

I'll show you the one upstairs. Oh, and I'd better shut the front door. I'll put it on the latch so that Robert can get back in.

Margery exits to the hall

Jaynie goes to the foot of the stairs. The front door slams

Margery appears. She picks up Jaynie's case and leads her upstairs

(*As they go*) I've put you two in my daughter's room. I hope you'll find it comfortable.

Margery and Jayne exit upstairs

Charles enters from the kitchen

Charles Gone! Thank God!

Charles exits to the kitchen, along the passage

Margery comes downstairs, picks up her cardigan, and exits to the hall

Charles enters from the kitchen carrying four wine glasses. He exits to the dining-room with them

Margery re-enters, picks up her shopping bag and exits to the kitchen

Charles re-enters from the dining-room carrying a pack of cigarettes. He crosses to the desk and empties them into a cigarette box, then exits to the kitchen, along the passage

Margery enters from the kitchen through the sliding doors and collects the wine bottles

Charles enters from the kitchen

Margery I've got the wine.
Charles Well done, darling. (*He stops and turns*) Margery!
Margery (*also turning*) Charles, where have you been?
Charles You're back!
Margery Don't be so obvious.
Charles My God, that was a narrow ...
Margery Narrow what?
Charles Narrow necks those Hock bottles have.
Margery Don't tell me you've never noticed that before. (*She moves towards kitchen, then stops*) And Charles, if you don't touch those roses again I'll give you a little surprise. And if you do touch them again, I'll give you a big one!

Margery exits to the kitchen

Charles goes to check on the front door

Charles (*turning away from the door, with eyes to heaven*) Thank you, Oh Lord, for leading me out of the valley of the shadow of death, into ...

At that moment, Robert rushes in hurls a coat over Charles's head and starts to bundle him off

Robert Sorry about this, but there's not a second to lose!

Charles (*disentangling himself*) What the hell are you playing at?

Robert Good Lord! Sorry, old boy. I thought you were Jaynie.

Charles Flattery will get you nowhere.

Robert Then, where is she?

Charles Who?

Robert Jaynie, you blithering idiot!

Charles I thought she was with you. I thought you'd gone.

Robert Some ass had parked right up against my backside. Took me ages to get the car out.

Charles Then where is she?

Robert Who?

Charles Jaynie!

Robert That's what I was asking you.

Charles But don't you understand? Margery's back.

Robert Good God! She's probably hovering about outside somewhere.

Charles No, she's in the kitchen.

Robert Then why didn't you say so? Let's get her, quick!

Charles No, not Jaynie, Margery.

Robert Then where the hell is Jaynie?

Charles You could be right, she might be outside. You look there, I'll look in the loo.

Robert and Charles disappear into the hall

Margery enters from the kitchen obviously looking for something

Robert and Charles return. Robert leading

Robert Nowhere, absolutely nowhere!

Margery Hello, Robert dear. How nice to see you.

Robert Margery! (*He kisses Margery*)

Charles Yes, Margery. (*He also kisses Margery*)

Margery And what is nowhere?

Charles Nowhere?

Margery (*searching in the desk drawer*) Robert was saying something was nowhere.

Charles Ah, that. Well, nowhere is where . . .

Robert I was just saying that if I had to live in London, there's nowhere I'd rather live than here—absolutely nowhere.

Margery (*crossing to look on the table*) You obviously don't know London very well. I can think of thousands of places I'd rather live than here.

Charles Oh, so can I—absolutely thousands.

Margery Then why have you always said you'd rather live here than anywhere?

Charles That's what I've always *said*, but it isn't what I've always *thought*.

Robert (*hoping to change the subject*) I'm sorry about Jane, Margery.

Margery Sorry? Why?

Robert Well, you see . . .

Margery Ah, there it is! (*She picks up a corkscrew from the drinks tray*) For your information, Charles, these bottles are screw-top. No, I think she's very attractive.

Margery exits to the kitchen

Robert Sorry, old boy, my fault.
Charles (*deep in thought*) What was?
Robert Corkscrew, I brought it in.
Charles Good idea. Corkscrew. Good idea. Look, did I hear right? Did I hear Margery say she thought Jane was very attractive?
Robert Come to think of it, that's what I heard her say.
Charles But Jane isn't here.
Robert That's true—Jane isn't here.
Robert }
Charles } (*together*) And Jaynie is!!
Charles (*panic starting*) You do realize what that means, don't you? They've met!
Rbert Yes, I do realize that, Charles.
Charles Margery and Jaynie have met.
Robert Yes, Charles. They've met.
Charles And you do realize that this could be the beginning of the end of my entire life—not to mention my marital bliss?
Robert Well, I realize it could be the end of something but just what, I'm not quite sure at the moment.
Charles (*pouring a drink*) Everything, I tell you, everything!
Robert (*taking the drink as though it were for him*) Thanks. Mind you, Margery's quite right.
Charles (*pouring another drink*) Margery's always quite right. What about, this time?
Robert Jaynie is very attractive. I was quite looking forward to driving her to the Savoy—never know what it might have led to.
Charles This is no time to think of fornication!
Robert You should have told yourself that in little old New York.
Charles Will you stop insinuating ...
Robert All right, all right. What puzzles me is her apparent lack of concern.
Charles Whose?
Robert Margery's. She just quite calmly said, "I think she's very attractive".
Charles That is Margery's deadly calm before her cataclysmic storm. Oh, my God! You must find out what she meant. You must find out!
Robert How?
Charles How do I know how? I don't know how. But you must do it now. Think how and do it now.
Robert Perhaps I could start by asking "How now, brown cow"?
Charles Oh, for God's sake!

Margery enters from the kitchen

Margery Dinner in about twenty minutes to half an hour. Is that all right?
Charles Lovely, darling, lovely. (*He kisses Margery*)
Margery (*crossing to Robert*) Here are some nuts to be going on with.
Robert Thank you, Margery.

Charles Yes, thank you, darling. Thank you. (*He kisses Margery again*)

Margery Charles, if you go on kissing me like that I shall begin to suspect something's wrong.

Charles Wrong darling? Nothing's wrong. Absolutely nothing. (*He indicates to Robert, "Now! Now!"*) I'm kissing you because I'm sorry about the potatoes. I forgot them. I'll go and do them now while Robert . . .

Margery Don't worry, I'll do this lot.

Charles What lot?

Margery Well, I presume those charred remains in the litter bin were once robust King Edwards.

Charles Yes. You see, when I said I forgot them, I meant I forget they were on.

Margery (*with a sweet smile*) Yes.

Margery exits to the kitchen

Charles (*calling after her*) That's what I keep telling you, darling, I'm no Fanny Craddock.

Robert More of a Fanny Hill. (*He sits*)

Charles Why didn't you help me?

Robert I can't even cook cornflakes.

Charles Not with the bloody potatoes! Why didn't you ask her?

Robert The opportunity didn't seem to present itself in the best of possible lights.

Charles I cannot remember a time when I felt more utterly miserable.

Robert I can't say that I'm exactly bubbling over with bonhomie.

Jaynie enters

Jaynie Do you know something? I am feeling just fine now.

Robert (*aside to Charles*) Of course! She'll tell us.

Charles What? Of course! Hello, Jaynie. Come and sit down and have a drink. (*He sits her in an armchair*)

Jaynie You mean I really can have one this time?

Charles What? Oh, very funny! Ha, ha, ha. That really is very funny! Isn't that funny, Robert?

Robert Hilarious.

Jaynie Scotch on the rocks, please.

Charles (*goes to the sofa table*) Scotch on the rocks it shall be. (*He picks up the gin bottle*) Now tell me, Jaynie . . .

Jaynie That's gin.

Charles What? Oh, so it is. (*He puts down the gin and picks up the vodka bottle*) Jaynie . . .

Robert And that's vodka.

Charles Surely not. Good gracious me. So confusing these damned labels. (*He finds the right one*) Now Jaynie, there was something I wanted to . . . that is, there was something Robert and I wanted to . . . the fact is, Robert wants to ask you something.

Robert Thank you—very much.

Jaynie Ask away, Robert.

Robert (*sitting on the desk*) Well, we understand that you and ... the wife have met.

Jaynie Sure thing. We've met. Could I have a little more ice, please?

Charles I'm so sorry. (*He gets more ice*) So, you've met?

Jaynie We have indeed.

Charles There you are, Robert, what did I tell you? They've met.

Robert Yes.

Jaynie And I must say I found her very charming.

Charles Did you? Oh good. But she is charming, very charming. But then you'd know that better than I, Robert—she being your ...

Rober What we meant was, what was her reaction to meeting you?

Jaynie Well, she didn't go out and ring bells or dance the hula-hula, but she seemed quite happy to see me.

Charles She's not very good at the hula-hula. But then, you'd know that better than I, Robert ...

Robert She was happy to see you?

Jaynie Why, yes. All that fuss and bother about her finding it strange and odd. Nonsense! She obviously understands perfectly.

Charles Understands?

Jaynie Yes.

Robert (*to Charles*) Wonderful thing, understanding.

Charles Yes. Wonderful.

Robert In fact, I can't understand people misunderstanding, can you?

Charles No, no. But I can understand people misunderstanding when they've misunderstood.

Robert Oh yes. That's very understandable.

Jaynie Well, I can't understand a word either of you is saying.

Charles Good. Well, there you are, you see. Politics.

Robert What do you mean, politics?

Charles I haven't the faintest idea. (*To Jaynie*) Nevertheless, Jaynie, when you say Margery understands, it might help to clarify things in my stupid, befuddled mind if you could elucidate a trifle as to precisely what extent she was able to nullify what—even under the most mitigating circumstances—might have conceivably been misconstrued as an embarrassing predicament.

Jaynie I got as far as "befuddled". Could you put the rest into English?

Robert (*spelling it out*) What did Margery say?

Jaynie She didn't say anything. Well no, that's ridiculous, of course she did. She came through the front door—(*to Robert*) because you'd left it open—just after I'd come out of the powder room. She said, "Hello", and I said, "Hello", and we introduced ourselves, and then we sat down. And then ... well, it was as if she'd been expecting me. (*She has acted out the moves and is now seated on the settee*)

Robert Expecting ...?

Jaynie She said she'd heard all about me. (*To Charles*) I didn't know you cared that much, Charlie. Then she offered me a drink—which I never got—and then (*to Charles*) she talked about you and roses.

Robert Rose's what?

Charles Robert!

Jaynie Then we had a chat about names and cooking fat . . .
Charles Cooking fat?
Jaynie Yeah, when she was at school.
Charles I think I've only got as far as "befuddled".
Jaynie It all arose because she thought my name was Jayne.
Robert Jane? (*To Charles*) JANE!
Charles Jane.
Jaynie Well, let's face it, it is Jayne really. I mean, that was my given name.
I became Jaynie because of . . . well, I don't know what because of—I just
did.
Robert I think you were right, Charles. I think Margery was understanding
because she misunderstood.
Charles Yes. And we mustn't allow her to misunderstand what she's
misunderstood.
Robert Most certainly not. But one thing above all is clear, and that is that
we understand where we stand.
Jaynie For Heaven's sakes! Is this some sort of English parlour game?
Robert In point of fact, yes. And it can be a very difficult one to play.
Charles Especially should the partners get muddled.
Robert Oh, my God! I hadn't thought of that!
Jaynie Can anyone play? I'm just crazy about parlour games.
Charles This one's enough to drive anyone crazy.
Robert (*suddenly, after a slight pause*) Good Heavens!!
Jaynie Oh!
Charles Don't do that, Robert. I nearly jumped out of my skin. Though,
come to think of it, I could do with someone else's right now.
Robert I'm sorry, but I suddenly remembered. Those tickets you wanted me
to collect.
Charles What about them?
Robert Well, it'll be too late to get them from the Box Office after dinner,
but I could drop a note into the theatre when I take Jaynie to the Savoy.
(*To Jayne*) You don't mind leaving a little early, do you?
Jaynie (*jumping up*) Dinner! Aren't I just too awful! I should be helping
Margery with the dinner. As for taking me to the Savoy, don't give it
another thought!

Jaynie exits to the kitchen

Robert Thank God for that!
Charles I may be saved!
Robert Thanks to me.

Margery enters from the kitchen and calls back to Jaynie

Margery Just put them on the hatchway. I'll pass them through later. (*To
Charles and Robert*) Come on you two, dinner is finally ready.

Margery exits to the dining-room
Jaynie enters

Jaynie And you don't have to take me to the Savoy anyway. Margery says
I'm staying here. I told you, she understands.

Jaynie exits to the dining-room

Charles You know what this means? According to Margery, Jaynie's sleeping here—with you!

Robert And according to Jaynie, she's sleeping here—with you!

Charles But that means you're sleeping with Margery!

The telephone rings sharply

Now who the hell is that? (*He turns towards it*)

Margery rushes in from the dining-room

Margery (*dashing to phone*) I'll get it! You start ladling the soup.

Charles and Robert go into the dining-room. They leave the door open and we hear the murmur of their voices

(*On the phone*) Hello? ... Speaking ... Who? Oh, hello. Just a moment. (*She runs quietly to the dining-room door and closes it gently*) Sorry—just turning off the radio ... Not at all, I'm delighted to hear from you. Where are you? ... At the Connaught. I'll just jot the number down. (*She does so on a jotting pad*) Got it. (*She puts the paper in ther pocket*) Well, I'm up to my eyes just now ... Yes, of course I'd love to, but this weekend is impossible ... To begin with, Charles is here ... Yes, and his brother and his wife are staying the weekend too, so I won't be able to spare a moment.

Charles opens the dining-room door and calls

Charles Come along, Margery. It's getting cold.

Charles goes back in to the dining-room

Margery Coming! (*Into the phone*) Look, I must fly. Why don't you give me a ring on Monday or Tuesday, and I'm sure we'll be able to arrange something ... That would be fine ... You do that ... Lovely ... Of course I do ... Of course ... Goodbye—Brad.

Margery puts the phone down, pauses for a moment and then turns to the dining-room door as

the CURTAIN *falls*

ACT II

The same. Just after dinner

Charles, Robert, Jaynie and Margery enter from the dining-room

Charles . . . and it poured and poured and poured. I've never seen such rain.

Robert I remember it raining like that once in Bradford—poured and poured and poured.

Jaynie It never rains in sunny California.

Margery Isn't that the title of a song?

Charles Why, so it is. (*He sings*) "California here I come . . ."

Margery No, I think that's a different one. Right then, Jaynie, how about you helping me with the washing-up while the men tell their dirty stories?

Charles (*falsely over-amused*) Dirty stories! Ha, ha, ha! Do you hear that Robert? (*He laughs far too long*)

Margery (*at last*) Oh, I didn't realize I'd just told one.

Jaynie whispers in Margery's ear

Of course, my dear, you know where it is.

Margery exits to the kitchen

Jaynie (*in embarrassment; to the men*) Freshen up.

Jaynie exits to the hall

Charles sinks into the armchair R,

Charles Oh, my God! That is the most exhausting meal I have ever had!

Robert I thought the duck was very good; but treacle pudding at this time of year was rather heavy.

Charles When we were first married, I foolishly told Margery I liked treacle pudding. I've had it once a week ever since for twenty years.

Robert Heavy . . . definitely . . . heavy.

Charles Actually, it wasn't the food I was referring to, it was the topic of conversation. Desperately trying to keep talking so as to prevent Margery asking awkward questions.

Robert No doubt about it, it was tough going. I don't suppose the weather has had such a run-down since they sent up the first satellite. (*He sits in the other armchair*)

Charles What I found tedious about tonight was that Jaynie would insist on playing footy-footy the whole damn time under the table. At one point she got her foot stuck right up my trouser-leg. After masses of heaving and pulling she finally got it free, and left a high-heeled shoe lodged half way up my calf. That's why I had to ask you to pour the wine—I was trapped!

Robert Good thing you did. I can just imagine Margery's face if she'd seen a female winkle-picker drop out of your trousers.

Jaynie enters

Jaynie Hi, I'm back.
Charles Ah. Did you have a good . . .? I mean, feeling fresh?
Jaynie Sure am. (*She pokes her finger in Charles' ear*) Ear tickle-wickle.
Charles Don't do that.
Jaynie You like it.
Charles Not after treacle pudding.
Jaynie (*presenting her behind to Charles*) Well go on, do what you do.
Charles Do what I do what?
Jaynie Do what you do with your hand.
Charles Do what I do with my hand?
Jaynie Yes, on my . . .
Robert I think I've suddenly remembered something I left in the car.
Jaynie (*stopping Robert*) No, you see, back home I used to say "Ear tickle-wickle" and do that. (*She puts her finger in her own ear*) And he would say "Hand smack-a-bum", and do that. (*She smacks her behind*)
Robert I see!
Charles Just harmless horseplay, you understand.
Robert Oh, of course.
Jaynie Well, go on, do it. (*She again presents her behind to Charles*)
Charles No, Jaynie.
Jaynie Oh, come on!
Charles No.
Jaynie Come on! (*She takes Charles' hand*) Hand smack-a-bum.
Charles (*freeing himself*) Jaynie, please! Margery may come out. (*He rises*)
Jaynie What of it? I told you, she understands.
Charles Possibly, but this might over-stretch her power of comprehension.
Robert (*rising*) Don't bother with him, Jaynie. Try it with me. If I let you ear tickle-wickle me, can I hand-smack-a-bum you?

Robert and Jaynie play the game. Jaynie squeals

Margery re-enters

Margery Charles, if you see Jaynie . . . Oh!
Robert Hello Marge, old girl, I was just . . .
Margery So I see.
Charles (*crossing to her*) It's the ear tickle-wickle hand-smack-a-bum syndrome.
Margery Is it?
Jaynie Oh, Margery, I hope you don't think I was taking advantage.
Margery Not at all, be my guest. I was wondering if you could help by passing the rest of the dishes through the hatchway?
Jaynie Sure thing.

Jaynie exits to the dining-room

Margery (*to Charles*) And don't let it give you any ideas.

Margery exits to the kitchen

Charles (*collapsing on to the sofa*) Oh my God! I feel as though I'm in one of

those torture chambers where the walls and ceiling are slowly closing in
on you.

Robert (*sitting next to Charles*) Well, before you get crushed to death what
are you going to do about Jaynie? It's getting nearer and nearer the time
when Margery thinks *I'm* sleeping with her, and Jaynie thinks you are.

Charles Yes, well I was giving that some thought over dinner. Margery had
arranged for you and Jane to sleep in Louisa's room; but there's also
Mark's room. So you can show Jaynie into Louisa's room and make sure
she sees you going into Margery's room—that will satisfy her. Then you
say goodnight to Margery and make sure she sees you heading for
Louisa's room—that will satisfy her. Then you tiptoe back to Mark's
room.

Robert I shall need a road map for that. And how will you explain to
Margery that you're going to sleep with Jaynie in Louisa's room?

Charles I won't have to. I'll undress in our room, tell Margery I'm going for
a pee, then pop into Louisa's room and tell Jaynie I feel sick and will only
disturb her, pretend to go into Mark's room, then double back to
Margery.

Robert You'll need a road map and the AA. And what happens tomorrow
morning over bacon and eggs when Jaynie asks if you're feeling better and
how lonely she was sleeping without you?

Charles She won't ask that.

Robert She might.

Charles You're right. She might.

Robert How about suggesting that Margery and Jaynie share one room
because you and I want to stay up late and talk?

Charles What are we going to talk about?

Robert We don't have to talk about anything, you idiot! Just sit up very
late—and get drunk, I would suggest.

Charles I can't see Margery falling for that. She's quite used to me going to
bed hours after her. I'm completely hooked on late-night movies, you
know.

Robert Well, for God's sake get completely hooked on some idea of what
we are going to do.

Margery enters from the kitchen

Margery Coffee's going to be rather delayed, I'm afraid. I think the
percolator's on the blink.

Charles (*rising*) That's all right, darling, because ... (*He has a sudden idea*)
Because Robert and I had thought it might be nice to take Jaynie for a
drink at the *Bull's Head*. (*He looks to Robert for support of his brilliant
idea*) Americans always like to see the inside of an English pub, and
you've never taken her to one, have you Robert?

Robert What? Er ... no.

Margery Do you think she'll like to see the inside of the *Bull's Head*?

Charles Of course—all the darts and shove-halfpenny, and what have you.

Margery It's all juke boxes and Space Invaders now.

Charles Even more unusual. Of course, you don't want to come, do you,
darling?

Margery Good heavens, no!
Charles Good.
Margery Oh, I don't know, though. It might be rather fun.
Charles No it won't, darling. It'll be ghastly. You'd hate it.
Margery Come to think of it, there is something else I want to do . . . ought to do.

Jaynie enters from the dining-room

Jaynie I think that's the lot. Now I'll help you with the drying-up.
Margery Oh, bless you.

Margery and Jaynie exit to the kitchen

Robert What's the idea of dragging all the way out to the pub? We've got plenty to drink here.
Charles Anything to keep Margery and Jaynie separated. I don't even like the idea of them being in the kitchen now. I know that, before long, someone is going to drop the most frightful clanger. (*He sits on the settee*)
Robert You could be right. And while we're there, we might be able to evolve some scheme whereby she can be persuaded to go to the *Savoy* tonight. That's it! Why don't you tell Margery you're going to watch the late-night movie, then, take Jaynie to the *Savoy*, do what you have to do, and when she's asleep, slip back here? I'll watch the movie and tell you all about it. Then you'll have a perfect alibi.
Charles In the first place, what will Margery think of you watching the late-night movie here, while your supposed wife of three weeks' standing elects to sleep at the *Savoy Hotel?*
Robert I suppose I could always watch it there. But that would mean booking a room—can't afford that.
Charles Secondly, it may surprise you to hear that I do not want to "do what I have to do", as you put it. I keep telling you it wasn't like that.
Robert And I keep telling you I don't believe you.
Charles (*rising*) In any case, the whole scheme is fraught with impossible difficulties. Unless . . . now wait a minute! I think my addled old brain has come up with a water-tight solution!
Robert Spill it.
Charles We'll take Jaynie to the pub, and while we're there, I will tell her that I think it would be much more romantic to spend the night at the *Savoy Hotel*. We'll come back here, and I will get Margery on one side and tell her that you and Jaynie think it would . . .
Robert (*rising*) . . . be much more romantic to spend the night at the *Savoy Hotel*. This is good, it's very good.
Charles We will then all start to watch the late-night movie, whereupon Margey will go to bed.
Robert Then you and Jaynie whip off to the *Savoy*! It really is very good!
Charles Meanwhile, you will drive to Wandsworth Common, or some place, and spend the night in the car there.
Robert Not so good.
Charles After half an hour, you ring me at the *Savoy*. I will tell Jaynie it was

Margery saying that you've been taken terribly ill, and carted off to hospital.

Robert After a night in the car on Wandsworth Common, that could be true.

Charles I will then do the noble thing and tell Jaynie I must go home and comfort the distraught Margery.

Robert So you spend the night in your bed here?

Charles Yes.

Robert And Jaynie spends the night in her bed at the *Savoy*.

Charles Yes.

Robert And I spend the night on Wandsworth Common?

Charles Yes.

Robert It's getting less good as it goes along.

Charles At seven o'clock tomorrow morning you phone here and ask to speak to Margery.

Robert Seven o'clock!

Charles Yes. Must be early, so that Margery is still drowsy.

Robert I don't suppose I'll have slept anyway.

Charles You tell Margery that you've heard from Cambridge that your mother-in-law's leg is worse, and that you've got to go up there straight away.

Robert Margery doesn't know about my mother-in-law's leg.

Charles All the better, make it her back, or a broken neck. You then drive to Cambridge to your real wife, and we'll see you both some other time.

Robert What happens when Jaynie phones tomorrow enquiring after my health?

Charles I'll make sure I answer the phone, and keep her at bay until after Tuesday.

Robert (*musing*) All night in the car on Wandsworth Common. You don't think you're stretching brotherly love just a little too far?

Charles Good God! I've told you I'll take you to the theatre!

Robert Oh yes. *The Day Before Yesterday*. Thanks.

Charles (*leaping into action*) Let's get going!

Charles leads Robert towards the hall

Robert There is one snag, old boy.

Charles What?

Robert You say you'll see me and my real wife some other time.

Charles Of course. Spend the weekend. Any time you like.

Robert It won't work. Margery is bound to see the difference between Jane and Jaynie.

Charles Oh, we'll cross that bridge when we get to it. I'll think of something.

Robert Could you make it Hampstead Heath that time?

Margery enters, followed by Jaynie

Margery Sorry we've been such ages. It all took longer than I thought, and we've been chatting away like nobody's business.

Charles That's what I was afraid of.

Margery What?

Charles That we might be too late for the pub.
Jaynie I can't wait to see a real English pub!
Robert Have they got any on Wandsworth Common?
Charles (*with a searing look*) Come along, then. Off we go! (*He quickly kisses Margery*) Sorry you can't come, darling.

Charles, Robert and Jaynie exit by the front door

Margery watches them through the window for a moment. She then moves to the desk and takes out the piece of paper she had written the telephone number on. She dials the number

Margery (*into the phone*) Connaught Hotel? Mr Denyer, please, Mr Brad Denyer . . . Mrs Fleminge. He's gone out? Oh . . . No, I'll ring later.

She replaces the receiver, pauses a moment and then moves the roses from the sofa table to the desk

The front doorbell rings, and at the same time the furious barking of a large dog can be heard

Margery exits to the front door

(*Off*) Go away . . .! Shoo! . . . Go away!!! GO AWAY!!! Look, come in, and I'll shut the door, then he'll stop.

The door is heard closing. The dog stops barking

Margery enters, followed by an attractive Girl in her early twenties, carrying a case

That's better. I'm sorry about that. Our neighbour's dog. They will let it out into the front garden, and it terrorizes the life out of anyone who comes near our front door.
Girl Very useful if it happens to be an unwelcome visitor.
Margery Yes, but it never works that way. Whenever salesmen or flag sellers come to the door the dog is in the back garden.
Girl Such is life!
Margery Yes.
Girl I'm sorry just to turn up like this . . .
Margery That's quite all right. Can I do something for you?
Girl I beg your pardon?
Margery Are you lost? Or do you want to use the loo? Please don't be embarrassed about it if you do. I'm constantly knocking on people's doors when I get caught short. Nothing would induce me to go to a public lavatory—not in these liberated days. It's next door to the front door. Oh, but there's no towel. I'll run and get one.
Girl No, please! It's not that. Isn't he here yet?
Margery Isn't who here yet?
Girl (*slightly flustered*) Oh, good Lord! Don't tell me I've come to the wrong house! This is Mrs Fleminge, and you are eighty-four? I mean . . . this eighty-four, and you are . .?
Margery Mrs Fleminge, yes. I only look eighty-four!
Girl I'm sorry about that. So Bobby hasn't arrived?

Margery Bobby?

Girl Bobby Fleminge—your brother-in-law. I was supposed to come here with him. Then, at the last minute I couldn't. My mother had an accident and I had to dash up to Cambridge. But it turned out to be nothing serious, so I thought I'd come straight back. I would have phoned to warn you, but I hadn't got the number.

Margery (*slightly puzzled*) Oh, that's all right.

Girl Bobby was so keen for me to meet you—and, of course, vice versa.

Margery (*sceptically*) Of course.

Girl Trust him to be late.

Margery Oh, but he's not. He got here just after seven.

Girl Oh, good. It would have been so embarrassing to have to introduce myself.

Margery No, please don't be embarrassed ... because I'm afraid you're going to have to.

Girl I'm Jane.

Margery Jane?

Girl Your sister-in-law. Bobby's number two.

Margery (*very bewildered*) Bobby's number two—I see. How silly of me, I should have realized at once. How do you do, number two. I'm Charles' number one.

They shake hands

Girl Margery.

Margery That's right, Margery. How clever of you to guess.

Girl Bobby told me.

Margery Yes, of course, he would have done, wouldn't he? Excuse me. (*She runs up to the window*)

Girl Is anything the matter?

Margery Not at all. I thought there was someone at the porch, driving up in a car. But it must have been another car at another porch. (*She crosses back to the Girl*) So, you're Jane.

Girl Yes.

Margery And you're not called Jaynie?

Girl No.

Margery Ah! What a pity you can't stay.

Girl Can't I?

Margery Didn't you say you had to fly?

Girl Not that I can remember.

Margery Good Lord, I must be hearing things. I could have sworn you said, "Good Heavens, is that the time? I must fly".

Girl No, I ...

Margery I know what it was, lie. Lie, not fly. I must lie ... I mean, you must lie ... lie down. You must be worn out after that terrible journey. I find flying so exhausting, don't you?

Girl I came by train.

Margery All the way from Portofino? How ghastly for you.

Girl No, all the way from Cambridge.

Margery Even further! I'm not surprised you want to lie down.

Girl But I don't want to ...

Margery I know, you don't want to bother me. It's no bother at all, I assure you. You can go in Louisa's room. No—Robert is in there. You wouldn't want that, would you?

Girl Well, I can't see any reason ...

Margery No, of course you can't neither can I—good thinking. I've got it! Our room. You can lie down there. Or how about a bath? That's it. Have a jolly good soak in the bath, and a jolly good lie on the bed. That should give me plenty of time.

Girl Plenty of time for what?

Margery To prepare Robert for the shock ... er ... the surprise he's in for, and get rid of her.

Girl Get rid of who?

Margery Did I say get rid of someone? How thoughtless of me. No ... er ... it's Charles. A friend of his. Well, not a friend, a partner—business partner. Frightful woman! American. She's his American affair ... er ... she deals with his American affairs ... that is ... well, I couldn't bear you to meet her, and nor could you. She might say the most frightful things and ruin your weekend. So, you can keep out of the way. That way, there'll be no way she can get in your way—and we won't have to think of another way.

Girl I see. Well, all things considered, I suppose that's the best thing to do.

Margery And how clever of you to think it up. What a sensible girl you are. You know, the moment Robert told us about you, I said to Charles, "Now that sounds a really sensible girl". How right I was.

The dog is heard to bark and Margery glances out of the window

Oh, Good Lord, they're here! Quick! We don't want to spoil Robert's surprise, do we?

Girl You will send him up, won't you?

Margery I most certainly will!—I mean, when the coast is clear.

Margery drags the Girl to the foot of the stairs

It's the first door on the right, and the bathroom's next door. The pink towel's the clean one. Or it might be the yellow—unless I put the green one there.

The Girl exits into the hall

Margery grabs the Girl's case and follows her off

The front door is heard to open. The dog barks furiously until the door is shut

Charles enters, followed by Jaynie and Robert

Charles Really, the neighbours must do something about that damn dog. Sorry about the pub, Jaynie. Perhaps it wasn't such a good idea after all, I'd forgotten it would be so crowded on a Friday night.

Jaynie Oh, that's OK. We nearly got in. Are all the bars that crowded in England?

Robert Yes, on a Friday.

Charles And on a Saturday.

Robert It's an old English custom. Every Friday and Saturday the entire population of the country cram into the local for a drink.

Charles It's our way of getting to know each other.

Jaynie When you're that crowded you can't help but get to know each other. I'll swear I could have sued six guys for breach of promise.

Robert It's also a test of our English manhood to see if one can get to the bar before the place closes.

Jaynie Well, you managed that, Bobby, so I guess you must be pretty virile.

Charles Oh, he's that all right.

Robert At any rate, I prove it legally.

Charles Yes, well . . . why don't we all sit down?

Jaynie Sure thing. All that walking. I'm exhausted. (*She flops into an armchair*)

Robert Oh, I enjoyed the walk. Helped to dissipate the treacle pudding. (*He sits in an armchair*)

Charles also sits

Jaynie How you English walk so far I shall never know.

Robert Yes, must have been all of five hundred yards.

Jaynie It was a quaint little place, though. Are all English pubs as old as that?

Robert No, some were built *before* nineteen-thirty.

Jaynie Gee! So, when are we off to the *Savoy*, Charlie?

Charles Ah, well, as I told you in the pub, I thought we'd watch the late-night movie first.

Jaynie We could watch it at the *Savoy*.

Charles Good Lord, no. We wouldn't get there in time.

Jaynie Surely it can't take till midnight to drive to the *Savoy*?

Charles What? Oh, I see what you mean. No, our late movie starts at half past ten.

Robert It's not a late late movie, it's an early late movie.

Jaynie Sure is. Back home our matinée movies don't finish till then.

Charles So we'll watch it here, all together. Much more fun. Don't you agree, Robert?

Robert Oh yes, much more fun.

Margery enters

Charles and Robert rise

Margery What will be?

Charles Margery! I never saw you.

Margery You wouldn't unless you had X-ray eyes. I was upstairs. And what will be much more fun here?

Charles We're all going to watch the late-night movie.

Margery I see.

Charles But you won't want to, will you?

Margery No.

Charles I thought not. Look, Margery, I'll come and help you with the coffee. There's something I want to tell you.

Margery It'll have to wait. I want to talk to you for a moment, here. You too, Robert.

Robert I'm all ears.

Margery You should consider yourself lucky they haven't burnt off.

Robert Eh?

Margery (*to Jaynie*) And I'm afraid you can't sit in that chair, Jaynie.

Jaynie (*getting up*) Oh dear, I'm sorry. Is it broken?

Margery No. You can't sit anywhere in this room. In fact, I must ask you to vacate this room altogether. It's a lovely evening, so I suggest you go and sit outside. You'll find a garden seat down by the rhododendrons.

Margery leads Jaynie towards the french windows and hands her a magazine

Here's something for you to read.

Jaynie (*reading the title*) "Scrambling with your Motor Cycle".

Margery My son gets it every week. He's very keen on horses.

Jaynie exits, propelled off by Margery

(*Turning to the men*) Now, then!

Charles (*rising to her*) Margery, I know that tone. You adopt it every time I've committed a domestic blunder. If it's the potatoes . . .

Margery It isn't the potatoes, Charles. In fact, for once, it's not you.

Charles (*surprised*) Oh! (*He turns towards Robert*)

Robert Not me, surely. I haven't done a thing.

Margery That remains to be seen. (*She clears her throat*) Not half an hour ago, Robert, while you were all at the *Bull's Head*, Jane arrived.

Robert (*rising*) Did she! (*He pauses*) Jane?

Charles Jane?

Margery Jane.

Robert Where is she?

Margery Having a bath.

Robert Having a bath? Jane?

Charles Jane?

Margery Jane, your wife—at least, that is the assumption I draw. But then, earlier I had drawn the assumption that Jaynie was your wife.

Robert looks to Charles, who looks away as though watching an intruding butterfly

Robert Yes. Well, the fact is, Margery . . .

Margery The fact is, Robert, that both these women claim some close relationship with you. Since I cannot believe that even you would be so foolish as to marry two wives in the space of three weeks, I have been forced to come to a very unpleasant conclusion.

Robert Margery, please listen . . .

Margery And that conclusion is, that, thinking your real wife to be in Cambridge tending an ailing parent, you elected to bring a . . . substitute to my house and pass her off as your wife.

Robert For God's sake! (*To Charles*) Charles, say something!

Charles (*with devastating calm*) I was hoping Margery wouldn't find out, old boy.

Robert What! (*Raising his voice*) Of course you were bloody well hoping Margery wouldn't . . .!

Margery No language, please Robert, and no hysterics. (*To Charles*) I can't say that I condone your collaboration in this sordid plan, Charles . . .

Charles mouths but doesn't utter

. . . but since Robert is your brother, I felt the least I could do was save him as much embarrassment as possible.

Charles Damn decent of you, Margery.

Robert Charles!

Margery I therefore told Jane that Jaynie was, in fact, an acquaintance of yours.

Charles Very consid . . . What?

Margery (*to Charles*) I told her that Jaynie was in the same business as you, and was part of your American affairs.

Robert (*shouting*) Part of them! She is . . .!

Margery I have asked you not to shout, Robert.

Charles (*aware of the open french windows*) Quite. Don't shout, Robert!

Robert (*to Charles*) Is that all you can say? "Don't shout Robert!"

Charles (*as though pleading*) I could also say that the fat may be in the fire, but the cat's not out of the bag.

Robert (*vehemently*) And your cow's jumped over the moon!

Margery I am now going up to my room to give you time to sort this out between you. (*She goes to the foot of the stairs and turns*) I am very happy to entertain your wife under my roof, Robert, but not your wife and your mistress—at least, not at the same time!

Margery exits upstairs

Robert turns on Charles, who darts away

Robert You bastard! You utter bastard!

Charles Now Robert, keep calm. Just keep calm. I am absolutely convinced this whole thing can be sorted out in no time.

Robert (*advancing on him*) And to whose advantage, may I ask? You not only connived to make Margery believe that your . . . "lay" is my wife, but you have now corroborated that she is, in fact, my mistress!

Charles I haven't done anything of the sort.

Robert Oh no? Then what the hell have you done?

Charles Can I help it if Margery's got hold of the wrong end of the stick?

Robert She's only done that because you're scared out of your jockey shorts she'll get hold of the *right* end of the stick.

Charles Y-fronts, actually.

Robert I don't care if it's a truss! Which, my God, you're going to need if you don't get me out of this—and that doesn't include a night on any blasted Common.

Charles What can I do, for heaven's sake?

Robert Do? You can tell Margery the truth, that's what you can do.

Charles I told you, she'd break her heart.

Robert You also told me she'd break your neck. That's what you're really afraid of.

Charles And all this because your wife has the same name as my . . .

Robert Go on, say it, "lay"—your "lay".

Charles Don't call her that!

Robert Concubine then, mistress, PICK-UP!

Charles (*at the french windows again*) Careful, old boy, she might hear you.

Robert What the hell does it matter? She knows what she is. She's the only one in this house who isn't pretending to be something else.

Charles Why did Jane have to turn up!

Robert (*sitting*) Why did Jaynie? At least Jane was expected.

Charles It's having the same names that's caused all the confusion. Why couldn't you have married someone called Mary, or Rosalind, or Abigail.

Robert I did marry someone called Abigail.

Charles Then why the hell didn't you stay married to her? She was a lovely woman. Only today I was saying to Margery, "Why didn't Robert stay married to Abigail? Lovely woman".

Robert Have you taken leave of your senses? You know perfectly well that, at this point in time, the only thing to be said in favour of Abigail is her name. And she didn't have anything to do with that.

Charles If she had, she'd have probably called herself Jaynie, just to spite me.

Robert Anyway, why do you keep putting the blame for this catastrophe on me?

Charles Because it's your fault.

Robert My bloody fault?

Charles Yes, your bloody fault! You should never have come for the weekend. Nobody asked you.

Robert You asked me!

Charles You could have refused, couldn't you?

Robert I wish to God I had.

Charles And to cap it all, you have to bring that . . . that *woman* with you called Jane.

Robert (*rising to him*) Don't you refer to my wife as a woman! I've had enough of your teetering tantrums and your conniving conspiracies. If you can't control yourself, I shall be compelled to strike you—something I have never done in my life.

Charles (*sitting*) Oh yes, you have. In the swimming baths—when you were ten.

Robert I was practising my breast stroke.

Charles You didn't hit me in the breast, you hit me in the ba . . .

Robert It was an accident.

Charles Accident or not, it very nearly prevented me passing from adolescence into manhood.

Robert If it had, you wouldn't have been able to shack up with Jaynie in New York, and we wouldn't all be in this current chaotic shambles.

Charles I do wish you wouldn't use that expression, "shack up". It puts a perfectly sordid inference on what was a very tender relationship.

Robert So you did shack up with her!

Charles I never said that! You deliberately misunderstand me.

Jaynie enters from the garden

Jaynie Isn't the movie started yet?

Charles No, Jaynie. (*Trying to urge her outside again*) We'll tell you when.

Jaynie But it's getting cold out there.

Charles There's an anorak in the garden shed. I'll fetch it for you. (*He crosses to her*)

The Girl enters, carrying her suitcase

Robert sees her

Robert Jane, darling!

Girl Hello, Robert. Goodbye! (*She turns towards the front door*)

Robert (*stopping her*) What are you doing?

Girl I came out of the bathroom just in time to hear Margery say that she was not prepared to entertain your mistress under her roof. I find I have every sympathy with her, so I'm leaving!

The Girl exits

Robert runs after her

Robert (*as he goes*) Jane!!!

The front door is heard opening

Jaynie For heaven's sakes! What was all that about?

Charles (*slightly stunned*) That was ... that was ... I think there has been a considerable impasse.

Jaynie That lady was angry.

Charles Yes, that lady certainly was ... angry. And I'm afraid it means, Jaynie, that our plans for the *Savoy* may have to be altered.

Jaynie In what way?

Charles Completely. In fact, we must put them off.

Jaynie Off! Why?

Charles Because ... Oh dear, I don't know how to tell you this. It's pretty sordid, and you're such a sweet, pure, innocent thing ...

Jaynie I can take it. Remember I live in California.

Charles seats Jaynie in an armchair and sits on the arm of it

Charles Well, I'm not going to beat about the bush, Jaynie, I'm going to tell you straight out. That girl—who you saw being angry just then—that girl ... is Robert's lover.

Jaynie You mean ...?

Charles Yes.

Jaynie His mistress?

Charles (*rising*) I told you it was sordid. But I'm afraid, in England, some men do carry on like that.

Jaynie Don't kid yourself—it's the same in the States.

Charles You amaze me! All those good, clean, American guys.

Jaynie Some of them have dirty faces.

Charles I suppose it's the same the world over.

Jaynie And Robert brought this ...

Charles Jane, her name is. Funny—just like yours.

Jaynie And he's brought Jane here when Margery . . .?

Charles Yes. I think Jane was under the impression Margery was going to be away. That's why she's angry with Robert.

Jaynie I can imagine. All the same, it's Margery I'm sorry for. Her own husband entertaining his mistress in her house!

Charles I quite agree—terrible!

Jaynie Poor Margery.

Charles Exactly. Poor Margery. That's why I feel I ought to stay here and try and be of some comfort to her.

Jaynie (*rising to him*) Of course you must, lover.

Charles That's very understanding of you.

Jaynie (*sitting again*) And I'll stay, too.

Charles Ah . . . yes . . . well, of course. But don't you think it will be distasteful for you? I mean, his wife and his . . . *amour.*

Jaynie I'll do whatever you think best, Charlie.

Charles (*getting her to her feet*) Splendid! In that case . . .

Charles is cut short by voices off

Girl (*off*) No! No! No!

Robert (*off*) Well, I certainly don't think we ought to stand in the street screaming at each other like a couple of fish wives!

Charles (*panicking slightly*) I think it might be better if we left them to it. I'll get you that anorak.

Charles steers Jaynie into the garden

The front door slams

The Girl enters, followed by Robert

Girl It's pointless trying to deny it. My hearing was never faulty, and my eyesight confirmed it when I saw her . . . standing there. Margery had done her best to cover up for you, but as always, the truth will out.

Robert Jane, you have got the whole thing wrong.

Girl That's the remark of a guilty man if ever I heard one. Margery quite categorically said . . .

Robert I know what she said, but she's got the whole thing wrong, too.

Girl Really? And I suppose Charles has got the whole thing wrong, and the dog next door has? The only people who seem to have got the whole thing right are you and that . . . creature!

Robert We haven't got anything right! I never clapped eyes on her until today.

Girl Huh! Like you'd only "clapped eyes", I suppose, on that blonde bit who came up to us in Portofino and said you'd chatted her up in a restaurant in Wolverhampton.

Robert I didn't chat her up! I spoke to her for no more than three minutes. And I only did that because she was the only white person in the place. I began to think the company had sent me to Calcutta, not Wolverhampton.

Girl Please don't forget that my mother comes from Wolverhampton, and she is as white as the ace of . . . as white as the driven snow.

Robert It's because of your mother that all this trouble has arisen, anyway.

Girl And what has my mother got to do with your cavorting with an American tart?

Robert If your mother hadn't got pissed and fallen over the kitchen stove, you would have come here with me today.

Girl How dare you suggest that my mother gets drunk! She pulled a tendon at the back of her knee. You know she has bad knees. It was my duty to go and look after her.

Robert Don't tell me you're going to spend the rest of our marriage tied to your mother's hamstrings.

Girl What a beastly thing to say—what a really beastly thing! And what do you mean, the rest of *our* marriage? Are you planning a third one already? With *that* (*meaning Jaynie*) no doubt!

The Girl goes to leave, but Robert pulls her back and sits her down

Robert Look, I am fed up with this. I am not going to be party to this deception any longer. I am going to tell you exactly what the situation is. I am no longer going to protect my reprobate brother. I am not going to have my marriage wrecked just because he's in danger of wrecking his own. So listen, Jane, and listen hard, because this is the complete truth . . .

Charles rushes in from the garden

Charles Sorry, old boy, but I am absolutely bursting! And I don't want to poison Margery's roses.

Charles exits to the hall

Robert Where was I? That "American tart", as you put it—though God knows she's as innocent as a flea on a koala bear—is, in fact, Charles' *affaire*.

Girl What!

Robert He picked her up in New York, and spent an illicit fortnight with her, whilst telling Margery that he'd been delayed on business.

Girl That's a bit old-fashioned.

Robert He thought he'd got shot of her. And then, out of the blue and totally unheralded, she suddenly turns up here, not three hours ago. If the whole of Skylab had landed on Charles's head he couldn't have been more pole-axed.

Girl She just turned up . . . here?

Robert Yes. And before I knew what had happened, I was inextricably involved.

Girl She just turned up, here, knowing that Margery . . .

Robert Ah, well, that's the whole point. Charles had told her . . .

Charles re-enters

Charles Ah, that's much better! Sorry, won't interrupt again.

Girl (*suddenly bursting into copious tears*) Oh Bobby, I'm so sorry. I'm so terribly sorry!!

Robert (*taking her in his arms*) Pussy-bags!

Girl I'll never forgive myself. I'll just never forgive myself!

Robert There, there, Jane darling. Oh, my lovely little peek-a-peek-a-peek-a-peek-a-boo.

Charles (*who has stopped at the french windows*) Anything wrong?

Robert Nothing more than you can see for yourself.

Charles Not my fault, I trust?

Robert What do you think?

Charles Not because I had to have a . . . surely?

Girl What a beast I am. How could I ever have said those horrible things!

Robert I said horrible things too, darling. I know your mother doesn't drink—that much.

Girl Yes she does. She drinks like a fish!

Charles I don't think fishes actually drink, you know. The water sort of goes through their gills . . .

Robert Charles, for God's sake!

Charles What I really meant to say was, how about a brandy?

Robert That's the first good idea you've had today.

Charles I'll get it.

Charles exits to the dining-room

Robert (*to the Girl*) You love brandy, don't you darling? It's the one little drinkie you really adore, isn't it?

Girl Yes, I do like brandy.

Robert And no more tears, please, darling. The one thing we've all been trying to do is to keep this ghastly thing from Margery. I'm sure you agree with that, don't you darling?

Girl Oh, I do. I most certainly do. Poor Margery.

Robert Exactly. So, no more tears. You'll feel fine after you've had a brandy.

Charles re-enters

Charles Terribly sorry, no brandy.

Robert (*rising*) Oh, God!

The Girl howls again

You'd better get something if you want this day saved.

Charles How about whisky?

Robert No, she hates whisky. Brandy's the only drink she really likes. I'll go and buy a bottle.

Charles The shops are shut.

Robert Isn't there an off-licence?

Charles Wait a minute! The Indian place. They sell everything, and they're open twenty-four hours.

Robert Where is it?

Charles Well, you know the pub we went to?

Robert Yes.

Charles Well, it isn't there. In fact, it's in the opposite direction.

Robert Turn right, out of the house, not left?

Charles That's it. Go for about . . . oh, I don't know, and you'll come to a cross-roads. Go over the cross-roads . . . No, it's better if you turn right.

Then take the first on your left. But it isn't *quite* the first—there's a sort of other left, but don't take that. Or, if you do, you branch right at a . . .

Robert Look, why don't I buy a bottle at the pub?

Charles They won't sell it to you. Besides they charge a fortune.

Robert I'll pay if you're so ruddy mean!

Charles Much better get it from the Indian place—and they have a wider selection.

Robert Good Calcutta-type brandy, I suppose.

Charles It's perfectly simple. Go out of the house and turn left . . .

Robert You said, right.

Charles That's right, right. Look, I'll come with you.

Girl (*still weepy*) I could do without a brandy, if it's going to be that much trouble.

Robert No, darling, I insist.

Charles So do I. I could do with one myself. Come on.

Robert exits

I haven't introduced myself. I'm Robert's brother, Charles. How do you do? Goodbye.

Charles exits

The front door slams

Margery comes downstairs carrying a hand towel, and Jaynie's case which she puts at the bottom of the stairs

Margery Was that someone going out or coming in?

Girl Going out. Robert and Charles have gone to get some brandy.

Margery Oh good, I'll put some in a cake I'm going to make for tea tomorrow. I have at last remembered the towel for the downstairs loo.

Margery exits to the cloakroom

The Girl makes rapid facial repairs

Margery enters

I hope you like cakes laced with alcohol.

Girl Oh yes, very much.

Margery Good. Dear me, the nights are beginning to draw in already. It's getting quite murky. (*She switches on the lights upstage and the table lamp*) If you'll excuse me, I'm going to start the preparations for my cake.

Girl Of course.

As Margery turns for the kitchen, Jaynie enters from the garden wearing an anorak

Jaynie Do I really have to stay outside any longer? I'm freezing.

Margery Oh, Jaynie! Good heavens, no. I've finished my little chat.

Jaynie Also, I'm being eaten alive by mosquitoes.

Margery I think you'll find they're midges. Just as irritating, but they won't give you malaria. By the way, do you two know each other?

Girl
Jaynie } *(together)* Well. . . .

Margery Jane, this is Jaynie. She's . . .

Girl I know.

Margery And Jaynie, this is Jane. She's . . .

Jaynie I know.

Margery Oh. Well, that's all right then.

Margery exits to the kitchen

There is an awkward pause as the two women survey each other, rather coldly

Girl *(moving away)* This is quite a situation, isn't it?

Jaynie Sure is. I have to hand it to those Fleminges. They're real understanding people.

Girl Well, Margery certainly is. I can't say I feel the same way about her husband.

Jaynie I agree. In fact, I'm surprised you came back after your walk-out.

Girl Robert wanted me to.

Jaynie And I suppose, if you love him . . .

Girl Of course I love him.

Jaynie And he loves you?

Girl Naturally. Mind you, I'm not suggesting that he doesn't feel badly about it all, but Charles is his brother, and he did stand by him during the divorce.

Jaynie Brothers do that, don't they? They're very loyal. I'm quite surprised he didn't marry again.

Girl What do you mean?

Jaynie Well, from what Charles told me, the divorce was some while ago. And yet, with his looks and what have you, I'm surprised he isn't married.

Girl But Robert is married.

Jaynie Oh, I know Robert is married. And I have to be honest, I'm not surprised you fancy him, despite that.

Girl Despite what?

Jaynie Despite the fact he's married.

Girl But he's married to me.

Jaynie He's what?

Girl Three weeks ago. Robert married me three weeks ago.

Jaynie Oh, you poor darling!

Girl I beg your pardon!

Jaynie He married you three weeks ago, and you didn't know that all the time he was . . .

Girl What are you talking about? Do you know something about Robert that I don't?

Jaynie Apparently, yes. Charles made it very clear to me that . . .

Girl Charles! The way he's carrying on, I wouldn't put too much reliance on what Charles says.

Jaynie Now wait a minute! Charles is a saint.

Girl You only say that because you're after him.

Jaynie And who wouldn't be?

Girl Any respectable woman wouldn't be!

Jaynie Now just let me get this clear. Either you are suggesting that only an unrespectable woman would go after Charles, or that I am unrespectable *for* going after him. Either way, I seem to come out of it pretty unrespectably.

Girl If the cap fits!

Jaynie Well, let me tell you this, Mrs Whited Sepulchre, I would rather be unrespectably going after a guy like Charles, than find myself hitched to a bigamist like his brother.

Girl Robert, a bigamist!

Jaynie I didn't want to tell you—I swear to that. Charles simply said you were Robert's girlfriend. Maybe that's what he still thinks you are.

Girl Don't be idiotic! Charles knows perfectly well Robert and I are married.

Jaynie He does?

Girl Of course he does. He sent us a wedding present.

Jaynie He did?

Girl A silver rose bowl inscribed, "To Robert and Jane. R.I.P." His rather tainted idea of a joke.

Jaynie He sent a wedding present to you and his brother, when all the time he was living in the same house as him and his other wife?

Girl What other wife, for Heaven's sake?

Jaynie Margery!

Girl Margery?

Jaynie Robert, who married you three weeks ago, is, and has been married to Margery for twenty years. They have kids, twins—not all that younger than me.

Girl (*after a pause*) Miss . . .?

Jaynie Jaynie will do.

Girl Jaynie. You have—with some reluctance, I admit—been endeavouring to break the news to me that my husband is a bigamist. I now have to break some news to you. Robert is not, nor ever has been, married to Margery.

Jaynie You mean they were living in sin?

Girl No. The only sinning in this household has been committed by the owner, Charles Fleminge. To what extent he has sinned, only his collaborator knows—and I'm sure you won't wish to tell us. I have this on the authority of the one person who should know—his wife, Margery.

Jaynie Are you telling me Charles is married to Margery?

Girl They are the ones with the twenty-year marriage certificate and twin children.

Jaynie (*subdued*) He told me he was divorced. (*She sits in an armchair*)

Girl He didn't!

Jaynie He did. He told me he was divorced.

Girl How could he!

Jaynie (*recalling it all*) In the *Pink Partridge*; not three months ago; table twenty-four; a Saturday night; we were having steak Diane with blueberry pie and whipped cream; the waiter came from Milan. (*She is near to tears*) At a quarter after midnight, Charles Fleminge—with an E—told me he was divorced.

Girl Don't upset yourself, my dear.

Jaynie He also told me . . . he also told me . . . (*Nearer still to tears*)

Girl Please, Jaynie, don't.

Jaynie (*tears suddenly gone*) The BASTARD!!! (*She rises*)

Girl That's better.

Jaynie The two-timing, double-faced, four-flushing son of a goddam whore-house bitch!

Girl That's much better.

Jaynie (*quiet again*) And I liked the guy.

Girl He's very attractive.

Jaynie I had quite something going for him.

Girl He has many most commendable points.

Jaynie I really dug him.

Girl He is quite diggable.

Jaynie And he's a shit.

Girl Yes, I'm afraid you're right.

Jaynie Wait a minute, does Margery know about Charles and me?

Girl Apparently not. For some time she thought you were me—got the names confused—and then she thought you were doing to Robert what, in fact, you were doing to Charles.

Jaynie I'm going to tell her! I'm going to tell her the truth.

Girl I don't think that would be very nice for Margery.

Jaynie You could be right at that. I'll kill that Charles. That's what I'll do— kill him!

Girl I don't think that would be very nice for Margery, either.

Jaynie But it's not right she should think I'm having an affair with your husband.

Girl It's even less right she should think you're having one with hers.

Jaynie That's true. No, it's better Margery knows nothing about it.

Girl I think so.

Jaynie But Charles isn't going to get away with this, you know. I'm going to fix that guy.

Girl Well, on the way, don't be too hard on Robert.

Jaynie OK, but he didn't deny being married to Margery when Charles told me he was.

Girl As you said, brothers are very loyal. Look, I'm going to unpack a few things. Do you want to come and talk to me while I do?

Jaynie Fine. (*Suddenly*) Jane! I've got it! I've just thought of something. I have the most incredible sleeping pills you have ever known—soluble partinitrates with Lethagon and PTQ—one, and your eyelids feel like iron curtains; two, and you hardly have time to take your clothes off. I'm going to drop a couple in Margery's coffee. Within five minutes she'll be yawning her head off and go up to bed. Then, I'm going to make up to Charles like something crazy, and when I've got him crawling on the ceiling, I'm going to tell that bum just what I think of him!

Girl Oh, to be a fly on the wall!

Jaynie Even better! Charlie says he's taking me to the *Savoy* after the late-night movie. Daddy said he'd look in there about that time. I shall introduce Charlie and say he seduced me against my will. If I know

Daddy, Charlie will finish up with two black eyes no steak in the State of Colorado will cure!

Girl (*shrieking with laughter*) Oh, no!

Jaynie (*as they start for the stairs*) After that, I shall go home to Mamma.

Girl Well, it makes a change to do that out of wedlock!

Jaynie and the Girl disappear upstairs

Silently, Margery slides through the french windows from the gathering dusk outside

She goes to the foot of the stairs, hesitates, then picks up Jaynie's case and is about to open it when she glances at the window

She quickly darts into the kitchen with the case

Charles and Robert enter. Charles carries a bottle of brandy

Robert I thought you said you knew where the place was.

Charles I was absolutely sure I did.

Margery enters from the kitchen, with the case

Robert It would have been quicker to have gone to India for it.

Margery replaces Jaynie's case where it was

Margery I hear you've been out to get some brandy.

Charles Yes, darling.

Margery (*drawing the curtains at the right-hand windows*) Fine, I'll borrow some for my cake.

Robert Jane was feeling a bit off colour, and brandy helps to pick her up.

Margery Oh, I think you'll find she's quite picked up now. (*She goes towards the stairs*) In fact, when she and Jaynie went upstairs just now, they were full of giggles. I'll tell them you're back.

Margery disappears up the stairs

Robert Full of giggles? What does that mean?

Charles No idea. I hope hysteria hasn't set in.

Robert And I hope this new plan of yours works out. Because if it doesn't Margery will have to go out and buy her widow's weeds.

Charles Fool-proof, old boy, can't fail. And it doesn't involve you at all. I explained the whole thing to Jaynie in the garden. We simply go back to square one. We *do* watch the late-night movie, and I *do* take Jaynie to the *Savoy*. But since Jaynie now thinks Jane is your girl-friend, you don't have to go to Wandsworth Common.

Robert Thank God for that.

Charles Once she's safely ensconced in room five hundred and four, I tell her—as, indeed, I have already hinted—that the situation between you and Jane and Margery is so tricky that I feel I must pop back and give you moral support.

Robert I thought you said it didn't involve me at all.

Charles Not actually, just metaphorically. The result of all this will be that everyone will finish up in the right bedroom without having to indulge in a French farce to get there.

Robert As I said before, I certainly hope—for your sake—that it works out.

Charles It will, old boy. I feel more confident now than at any point since Jaynie first darkened that front door. At long last, I feel I can see a dim light at the end of the tunnel.

Robert Let us hope it doesn't belong to an oncoming express!

Jaynie enters from the stairs, followed by the Girl

Jaynie ... I can't understand it, I could have sworn it was in the bathroom. (*She finds her suitcase*) Why, here it is all the time. (*She sees the men*) Oh.

Charles Hello, Jane ... Jaynie.

Jaynie (*putting it on*) Why Charlie, honey, where have you been? You left your little Jayniekins all on her lonesome, didn't you, sugar?

Charles (*slightly taken aback*) Did I? Yes, well you see, I had to ...

Jaynie Never mind. We're together again, that's all that matters, treasure. And now, will you excuse your baby, because she must just go and ...

Charles Freshen up?

Jaynie Why, yes! Must look my best for my lover boy, mustn't I?

Jaynie exits to the hall with her suitcase, giving the Girl a huge wink on the way

Robert Did I hear an engine whistle?

Charles What? I'll get the brandy glasses.

Charles exits to the dining-room

Girl I still can't tell you how sorry I am, Bobby.

Robert Forget it, darling, everything's going to work out fine. Charles has got a fool-proof plan for Jaynie.

Girl Really? Well, Jaynie's got a plan for Charles that's going to make him look a pretty good fool.

Margery comes downstairs

Margery Coffee everyone! It must be ready by now.

Margery exits to the kitchen

Girl I'll give you a hand, Margery.

The Girl exits to the kitchen also

Charles emerges from the dining-room with brandy glasses

Charles If I couldn't see that the seal on that bottle is unbroken, I would have said Jaynie had drunk half of it already. What the hell was she playing at? And in front of Jane, too. (*He gives Robert a brandy*)

Robert Charles, old boy, there's something I've got to tell you. That dim light at the end of the tunnel; it isn't an oncoming express, it's a laser beam!

Charles What are you talking about? (*He pours himself a brandy*)

Robert Jaynie ... (*He stops*)

Jaynie enters, looking rather puzzled

Ah, Jaynie! Feel nice and freshened up?
Jaynie (*subdued*) What? Oh yes. Thank you. (*She sits up in the armchair* R)

Margery and the Girl enter with coffee things

Girl Where do you want it, Margery?
Margery (*indicating coffee table near the settee*) Here, I think. I think we could do with those french windows closed now, Charles.
Charles Yes, of course, darling.
Margery (*as she pours*) I'll pour the coffee and you all help yourselves to cream and sugar and what-not.

The Girl is about to pick up a cup. Margery stops her

Margery No, dear, that's Charles's.

The Girls hands a cup to Jaynie and Robert. Charles sits on the end of the settee

I was saying earlier to Jane, wasn't I Jane? The evenings seem to be drawing in already, and yet it was only mid-summer's day a week ago.
Robert The whole weather spectrum seems to have changed radically in the last few years.
Margery So you were saying at dinner, Robert. Wasn't he, Jaynie?
Robert Was I?
Jaynie Yes. Yes, he was.
Margery Here's your coffee, Charles. I've sugared it for you.
Charles Thank you dear.
Jaynie I read somewhere that the change in the weather is due to the moon.
Girl (*sitting on the arm of Robert's chair*) I thought that was the change in the tide.
Jaynie Is that so? I knew it was the change in something.
Robert I think it's a great shame mankind ever landed on the moon.
Jaynie You only say that because we got there first.
Robert No, it's nothing to do with that. The dear old moon has lost its magic; we know too much about it now. It's not made of cheese, and it's not even round. It can't be nearly so romantic for young lovers to spoon under.
Girl Get that word, spoon! "Let us spoon 'neath the moon in the balmy month of June". They don't write lyrics like that any more—thank God!
Margery I think I still find it more alluring than, "Let's jig at the gig with the one that I most dig".
Jaynie Oh, I think I know that one.
Margery Do you? I've just made it up.

Charles has not engaged in the last exchange, but has concentrated on drinking his coffee—not unobserved by Margery

Margery Right, now. Has everyone got cream and sugar?
Girl (*rising with a sudden thought*) Oh, Jaynie, could I have some of your sweeteners instead of sugar?

Jaynie Er, yes, of course.

Girl Wouldn't you prefer sweeteners, Margery? They're brand new ones, and very effective.

Margery What a good idea. Yes, I think I would. Just a couple, that's all.

Girl That's all you need.

The Girl hands Margery's cup to Jaynie, then turns back to Margery so as to ensure Margery cannot see Jaynie putting two tablets into the cup. She gives cup to Margery and re-seats herself

Margery Thank you, dear. And where's this brandy we've all been promised?

Charles I'll get it. (*He makes two small efforts to rise out of the sofa, but fails*)

Robert Let me. (*To Charles, as he passes*) Old age creeping on?

Charles Must be, I think.

Margery You haven't got your "back" again, have you?

Charles No, it's not that . . .

Margery He's got the most awful "back", you know.

Jaynie Really? I sometimes get a "neck".

Margery Do you? I get a "head".

Girl My mother gets a "leg".

Robert I won't tell you what I get! (*He gives a brandy to Margery and another to the Girl*)

Margery (*to the Girl*) And how do you like our house, Jane?

Girl I think it's lovely, Margery.

Robert gives a brandy to Jaynie and stays by the desk

Margery We like it. This used to be two rooms, of course. We knocked it into one. I like through-rooms.

Jaynie Especially with the french windows—makes it so light.

Margery Charles was ribbing me about the french windows earlier, weren't you Charles?

Charles (*dazedly*) What?

Margery I told him he ought to use the back way into the garden, and he said, "What's the use of having french windows if you've got to go in and out the back way?"

Girl Does save the carpets, though.

Margery Exactly. That's why I used the back way just now, when I went to put the tea-leaves on the rose-bed. It was then that I heard raised voices.

Charles (*now quite sleepy*) Our neighbours are impossible. Damn dog, too.

Margery No, it wasn't our neighbours, Charles. It was our guests.

Charles Guests?

Robert Probably Jane and me, Margery. So sorry.

Margery No, not Jane and you, Robert. Jane and Jaynie.

Jaynie Me?

Margery I feel I owe you two an apology—especially you, Jaynie.

Girl You've done nothing to apologise to me for.

Jaynie Nor me.

Margery Oh yes, I have. As a result of a foolish misunderstanding on my

part, I jumped to the erroneous conclusion that you and Robert were . . .
well, closely acquainted.

Jaynie I only met him today.

Margery I know that, now. And, of course, I also know the real reason why
you are in this house.

Jaynie You do?

Margery Yes, I do. I was nearer the mark than I thought when I told Jane
that you were part of Charles's American affairs.

Robert (*aside to Charles*) I think it's the laser beam *and* the oncoming
express, old boy.

Jaynie Margery . . . I . . . I . . .

Margery My dear, I don't blame you—not in the least. There's absolutely
nothing wrong in showing affection towards a divorced man who is living
with this brother and sister-in-law and their two children in a quiet little
suburb in Surrey.

Jaynie (*rising, to Charles*) It is what you told me, isn't it, Charlie? That is
what you said.

Charles (*his eye-lids drooping*) Jaynie, I . . . (*He opens his mouth to say more,
but this develops into a massive yawn*)

Margery I shouldn't bother, dear. I think he's suddenly got very tired.
(*Rising*) Oh dear, we need some more cream.

Margery exits to the kitchen

Jaynie Charlie!

Girl (*crossing to Jaynie*) I think you've made the most terrible boo-boo.

Jaynie It's not my fault. I didn't do a thing.

Robert What's going on? What's happening?

Girl You put them in the wrong cup.

Jaynie I didn't put them in any cup. Those really were sweeteners. I
couldn't find the bottle.

The Girl sits

Margery enters from the kitchen with a small bottle of tablets

Margery Is this the bottle you've mislaid? I hope you don't mind, I
borrowed them. One, and your eye-lids feel like iron curtains; two, and
you hardly have time to take your clothes off. Since I didn't want Charles
to do that—especially in front of you—I gave him three.

Jaynie Oh dear.

Margery I also thought it might prevent him getting two black eyes.

The telephone rings. As Robert is nearest he answers it

Robert (*into the phone*) Hello?

Jaynie Margery, what must you think of me?

Margery My dear, I've told you. Under the circumstances, I don't blame
you in the least.

Robert (*off phone*) Anyone know someone called Bradley?

There is a pause. Margery is quite still

Margery Bradley? Are you sure it isn't Branchard—The people the children are staying with?

Robert (*into phone*) Excuse me, what was the name again? . . . Oh, I see. (*Off phone*) That was the first name. The other one is Denyer. And he wants to speak to . . .

Jaynie (*as though coming out of a trance*) Denyer? That's me. Bradley Denyer! That's my father!

Margery (*mildly pole-axed*) Your . . .!

Robert But he didn't ask for you, he asked for . . .

Jaynie moves towards the phone. Margery speaks quickly to stop her advance

Margery Take it in my bedroom, dear. It may be private. (*Into the phone, quickly, in almost a disguised voice*) She'll be right with you.

Jaynie runs up the stairs

(*Calling, to Jaynie*) First on the right!

Jaynie exits up the stairs

Jaynie (*off*) Thanks.

Robert Bradley Denyer? That name rings a bell.

Girl Not with me.

Robert No, it was some years ago. Racing motorist, or high jumper . . . or some sort of sportsman.

Charles (*through continuous yawning*) That's it . . . that's who it was . . . I've remembered . . . Brad . . . Brad Denyer!

Robert Of course! Tennis, very big stuff.

Charles Brad Denyer! Is he . . .? Is he . . .? (*He mimes "on the telephone" with his arm, but is too exhausted to say so*)

Robert I know why it rang a bell. I read something in the evening paper, in the pub, that he'd scratched from Wimbledon this year, suddenly. (*To Margery, who is staring straight ahead*) You must remember Brad Denyer, Margery? Marvellous player.

Margery Yes, I . . . I think I do.

Charles Of course you . . .! (*He nods off again*)

Margery (*quite quietly*) I didn't know he'd scratched from the tournament this year.

Robert Pity, really. Wimbledon won't be the same without him.

Girl I know who you're talking about, now. Getting on a bit, but very dishy?

Robert If you like that sort of thing.

Girl I do, that's why I married one.

Robert I don't know whether that's a compliment or not.

Girl (*to Margery*) And you mean to say that gorgeous hunk is the father of . . .?

Margery Yes . . . yes. (*Looking at Charles*) Ironical, isn't it?

Charles stirs, looks as if he is about to say something but relapses

Jaynie re-enters

Jaynie Well, what do you know!

Margery Everything all right?

Jaynie Sure thing. Though he seemed quite surprised to talk to me.

Margery Glad you hadn't gone out, I expect.

Jaynie Do you know what he said? He said he'd scratched himself, and would be flying home with me on Tuesday.

Margery That will be nice for you.

Jaynie Yeah. But it sure must have been a bad scratch if he has to leave that early.

Margery I'm sure he'll be all right. Did he say anything else?

Jaynie Something about, he was too old for the game anyway.

Margery I see.

Jaynie But what game?

Robert You mean you don't know?

Charles I know ... (*He yawns*)

Margery (*to Jaynie*) He could mean anything, my dear.

Jaynie Gee, I've just thought. How come he knew this number?

Robert That's a point.

Margery Oh ... er ... while you were at the pub I phoned the *Savoy* and gave it to them for you ... in case of any messages ... or anything.

Jaynie My, what a lucky thing you did!

Margery Yes, very lucky. And I must also admit that, after I'd "borrowed" your sleeping pills, I took it upon myself to order you a taxi. It should be here any time now.

Jaynie Oh, I see. Well, let me tell you this, Margery; I'm very glad you did.

Margery Yes, I'm very glad I did, too.

Jaynie I'll go and ... get ready.

Jaynie exits to the hall

Robert (*now feeling they are de trop*) Jane, darling, I think we ought to vacate the scene of action and retire to our quarters.

Girl Yes, I agree. Goodnight, Margery, and I hope you don't mind me saying so on so short an acquaintance, but I think you're a lovely lady.

Margery (*smiling*) Thank you.

Robert And I think you're lovely, too, old girl.

Margery Thank you—old boy!

Robert kisses Margery

The front doorbell rings

Charles (*waking up*) Hello!

Girl Would that be her taxi?

Margery I expect so. (*She looks at her watch*) Dead on time, too. How remarkable.

Margery starts to leave, but Robert stops her

Robert You know, I think we're all pretty glad you ordered it—one way or another.

Margery (*pointing to Charles*) How about him?

Robert Him? Oh, he'll be overjoyed. He's been trying to get rid of her all night!

Margery And, Robert, if you thought Brad Denyer asked for me on the telephone, you must have misunderstood.
Robert I understand. I misunderstood.

Margery goes off into the hall

Girl You know, I'm glad I married her brother-in-law.

Jaynie enters with her suitcase

Jaynie Was that my cab?
Girl Yes, so we'll say goodbye. In a way, it's been rather fun having you mistaken for me.
Jaynie Sure was great from where I was sitting.
Robert (*referring to the Girl*) Pity she turned up and ruined it all!
Jaynie Goodbye, Bobby.
Robert Goodbye, Jaynie. See you.
Girl Oh no you won't!

The Girl drags Robert upstairs

Jaynie wanders down to look at the sleeping Charles

Margery enters

Margery That, Jaynie, is your taxi, so you must be on your way now.
Jaynie Sure thing. (*She starts to go, then stops and crosses to Margery*) You know, since I've never been in this situation before—and pray God, never will be again—I just don't know what to say.
Margery Then let me say it for you. (*As it is now fairly dark outside she begins to draw the curtains of the french windows*) The joy of living is that you never grow too old for anything. That being the case, the surprises grow less surprising, and the shocks less shocking. (*She draws the downstage curtain of the french windows, then turns. The curtains are not quite closed*) So go back to your great big country, and live a great big life!
Jaynie I sure hope I do half as good as you have. (*Looking down at Charles again*) Say "Cheerio" for me, will you?
Margery Of course.
Jaynie You didn't give him more than three, did you? Could be dangerous.
Margery I'll remember that! By the way, I've told the taxi driver to take you to the Connaught Hotel—that's where your father is.
Jaynie Huh?
Margery Give him my regards, and tell him that, if I ever take up tennis, I'll see him in Forest Hills.
Jaynie I don't know what you're talking about but I'll tell him just that!

Jaynie exits

The front door shuts. Charles stirs in his sleep. Margery switches off the table lamp. She takes the slip of paper with Brad's number on it out of pocket and slowly crosses to the wastepaper basket

Charles Bloody Brad!
Margery Yes, my darling, bloody Brad. (*She tears up the slip of paper and*

drops it in the wastepaper basket) But Robert is quite right, you know. Wimbledon won't be the same without him. (*She crosses to Charles and kisses him on the brow*) Goodnight, my darling.

Margery switches off the main lights. The moonlight streams through the opening of the unclosed curtains and picks up the sleeping Charles and the roses on the desk. Margery turns into the hallway where there is light from the staircase

Charles Margery.
Margery Yes.
Charles The roses would look much nicer on the desk.
Margery (*after a slight pause, she smiles*) I know. That's why I put them there.

She turns to the staircase as

the CURTAIN *falls*

FURNITURE AND PROPERTY LIST

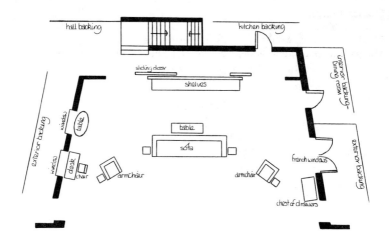

ACT I

On stage: Sofa
Sofa table
Two armchairs
Desk and chair. *On desk:* clock
Occasional tables. *On them:* ornaments, ashtrays, newspapers, a lamp, cigarette box
Hall rack and table in hall
Pictures on walls
Wastepaper basket
Telephone; jotting pad
Radiators
Shelves with hi-fi, books etc
Small chest of drawers
Magazine

*Set
off Stage:* Kitchen dresser, visible when kitchen door is open

Off Stage: Few pieces of cutlery **(Margery)**
Secateurs, bunch of roses, T-shirt bearing the slogan "Get with it, Daddy-O" **(Charles)**
Vase **(Margery)**

Shopping bag **(Margery)**
Cardigan **(Margery)**
Golf-clubs, handgrip **(Robert)**
Two glasses of scotch and water **(Charles)**
Whisky bottle, jug of water **(Charles)**
Case **(Jaynie)**
Ice bucket **(Robert)**
Tray of drinks, corkscrew, gin bottle, vodka bottle etc **(Robert)**
Two bottles of wine **(Margery)**
Four wineglasses **(Charles)**
Coat **(Robert)**

Personal: **Margery:** watch
Margery: duster
Charles: cigarette lighter

ACT II

Strike: Robert's golf-clubs and handgrip

Set: *In desk:* piece of paper

Off stage: Case **(Girl)**
Handtowel, Jaynie's case **(Margery)**
Anorak **(Jaynie)**
Bottle of brandy **(Charles)**
Brandy glasses **(Charles)**
Tray with coffee pot, cups etc **(Girl)**
Bottle of tablets **(Margery)**

Personal: **Jane:** make-up kit
Jaynie: sweeteners

LIGHTING PLOT

ACT I

To open: Effect of evening June sunlight

No cues

ACT II

To open: Evening sunlight, less bright than before

Note: Although not specifically indicated, there will be a general lessening of light from the apparent external light sources

Cue 1	**Margery** switches on main lights *Snap on interior lighting, including wall lights*	(Page 43)
Cue 2	**Margery** switches on practical table lamp *Intensify lights in area of lamp*	(Page 43)
Cue 3	**Margery** draws curtains at windows, R *Bring down all lights offstage right*	(Page 47)
Cue 4	**Margery** draws the curtains on the french windows *Slight fade of lights from offstage left*	(Page 54)
Cue 5	**Margery** switches off the table lamp *Bring down lights in area of table lamp*	(Page 54)
Cue 6	**Margery** switches off main lights *Snap off all interior lighting, apart from a spill from upstairs, intensify light through parted curtains, moonlight effect*	(Page 55)

EFFECTS PLOT

ACT I

Cue 1	**Margery** exits. **Charles** wanders about *The telephone rings*	(Page 5)
Cue 2	**Margery** dashes into the hall *The front door slams*	(Page 8)
Cue 3	**Charles** picks up roses and puts them into vase *The doorbell rings*	(Page 8)
Cue 4	**Charles:** ". . . how to get in touch with me" *The doorbell rings*	(Page 12)
Cue 5	**Charles:** "So you have." *The doorbell rings*	(Page 12)
Cue 6	**Jaynie** goes to the foot of the stairs *The front door slams*	(Page 20)
Cue 7	**Charles:** "But that means you're sleeping with Margery!" *The telephone rings*	(Page 26)

ACT II

Cue 8	**Margery** moves the roses from the sofa table to the desk *The doorbell rings and a dog barks*	(Page 32)
Cue 9	**Margery:** ". . . I'll shut the door, then he'll stop." *The door is heard closing, the barking stops*	(Page 32)
Cue 10	**Margery:** "How right I was." *Dog barks*	(Page 34)
Cue 11	**Margery** grabs case and exits *Door opens and dog barks until door is closed*	(Page 34)
Cue 12	**Robert:** "Jane!" *Door opens*	(Page 39)
Cue 13	**Charles** steers **Jaynie** into the garden *The door slams*	(Page 40)
Cue 14	**Charles** exits *The door slams*	(Page 43)
Cue 15	**Margery:** ". . . prevent him getting two black eyes." *The telephone rings*	(Page 51)
Cue 16	**Robert** kisses **Margery** *The doorbell rings*	(Page 53)
Cue 17	**Jaynie** exits *The front door shuts*	(Page 54)

MADE AND PRINTED IN GREAT BRITAIN BY
LATIMER TREND & COMPANY LTD, PLYMOUTH
MADE IN ENGLAND